D1370278

creating a
newsletter
in InDesign

Visual QuickProject Guide

by Katrin Straub and Torsten Buck

**Peachpit
Press**

Visual QuickProject Guide
Creating a Newsletter in InDesign
Katrin Straub and Torsten Buck

Peachpit Press
1249 Eighth Street
Berkeley, CA 94710
510/524-2178
800/283-9444
510/524-2221 (fax)

Find us on the World Wide Web at: www.peachpit.com
To report errors, please send a note to errata@peachpit.com
Peachpit Press is a division of Pearson Education

Copyright © 2005 by Katrin Straub and Torsten Buck

Editors: Doug Cruickshank and Nancy Davis
Proofreader: Ted Waitt
Production editor: Connie Jeung-Mills
Compositor: Owen Wolfson
Cover design: The Visual Group with Aren Howell
Cover production: Aren Howell
Cover photo credit: Photodisc
Interior design: Elizabeth Castro
Indexer: Julie Bess

Notice of Rights
All rights reserved. No part of this book may be reproduced or transmitted in any form by any means, electronic, mechanical, photocopying, recording, or otherwise, without the prior written permission of the publisher. For information on getting permission for reprints and excerpts, contact permissions@peachpit.com.

Notice of Liability
The information in this book is distributed on an "As Is" basis, without warranty. While every precaution has been taken in the preparation of the book, neither the author nor Peachpit Press shall have any liability to any person or entity with respect to any loss or damage caused or alleged to be caused directly or indirectly by the instructions contained in this book or by the computer software and hardware products described in it.

Trademarks
Visual QuickProject Guide is a registered trademark of Peachpit Press, a division of Pearson Education.

All other trademarks are the property of their respective owners.

Throughout this book, trademarks are used. Rather than put a trademark symbol with every occurrence of a trademarked name, we state that we are using the names in an editorial fashion only and to the benefit of the trademark owner with no intention of infringement of the trademark. No such use, or the use of any trade name, is intended to convey endorsement or other affiliation with this book.

ISBN 0-321-27892-5

9 8 7 6 5 4 3 2 1

Printed and bound in the United States of America

If everything you try works, you are not trying hard enough.

— Gordon Moore

Thanks

To the entire Peachpit team—in particular, to our editors Douglas Cruickshank and Nancy Davis for their dedication, as well as to Marjorie Baer for her continued trust.

contents

contents

introduction

The Visual QuickProject Guide that you hold in your hands offers a unique way to learn about new technologies. Instead of drowning you in theoretical possibilities and lengthy explanations, this Visual QuickProject Guide uses big, color illustrations coupled with clear, concise step-by-step instructions to show you how to complete one specific project in a matter of hours.

Our project in this book is to create a beautiful four-page newsletter using Adobe InDesign. You will set up the basic document, edit text, add color, place graphic elements, and add photos. You will also learn how to construct a table, set up styles, and print your work or export it for digital delivery.

There are hundreds of thousands of newsletters on every imaginable subject being produced every year. A newsletter is an excellent tool to get your message out and help you build or maintain relationships. This Visual QuickProject Guide shows you just how easily it can be done.

No matter what kind of newsletter you need to create—it can be anything from a holiday card to a company newsletter—this Visual QuickProject Guide shows you just how easily it can be done.

what you'll create

Draw lines and create colored background frames for the table of contents.

Create frames for your text, link them together, and fill them with place-holder copy.

Place, position, and adjust the masthead image and photo.

Determine styles and apply them to text frames.

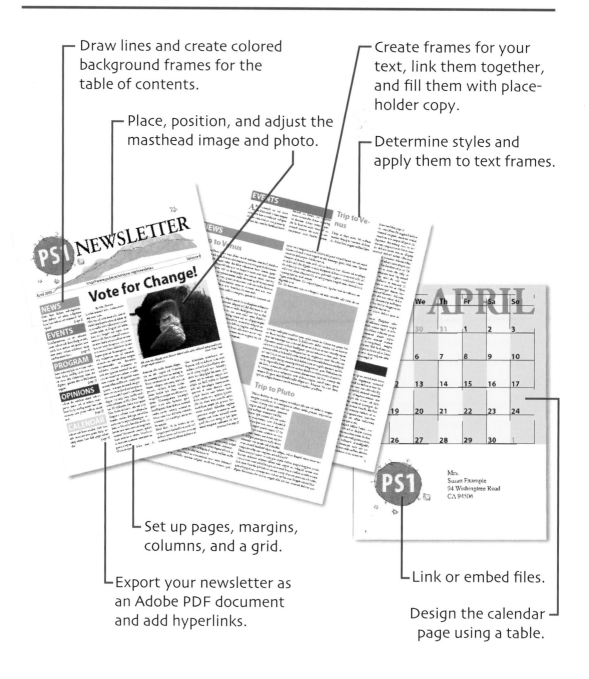

Set up pages, margins, columns, and a grid.

Export your newsletter as an Adobe PDF document and add hyperlinks.

Link or embed files.

Design the calendar page using a table.

useful tools

The desktop publishing program Adobe InDesign CS (Creative Suite) for Windows and Mac is the software used to create this newsletter. InDesign is the program of choice when it comes to handling text and layout. It is the most powerful program available. A significant benefit to using InDesign is that it is tightly integrated with other widely used applications such as Adobe Photoshop, Adobe Illustrator, and Adobe GoLive, all of which come in handy when you want to design or modify elements such as logos, photos, or illustrations or when you want to publish your newsletter on the Web.

You will need an image-editing application like Adobe Photoshop or Adobe Photoshop Elements if you are going to edit your photos or images in any way to prepare them for the newsletter. This includes retouching and resizing photographs and graphic images for your newsletter.

before you begin

Before actually creating the document in Adobe InDesign, you must make some decisions about your newsletter:

- What is the concept and content of your work?

- Who is the audience?

- What does your competition look like (if applicable)?

- What is your budget?

- How (and how often) do you plan to distribute the newsletter?

- How will you promote your newsletter?

- How will you get your readers' feedback?

Starting a project and learning a new software program are always a mix of fun and anxiety. Take your time and go through this book chapter by chapter. You will be rewarded with a solid sense of the basics and the ability to build on that knowledge with your unique designs. Keep up your optimism and good spirits. Most of all—enjoy!

the next step

Although this Visual QuickProject Guide gives you a solid understanding of what it takes to set up a newsletter, it does not explain design theories or the depth of Adobe InDesign. If you are interested in exploring InDesign in greater detail, check out InDesign CS for Macintosh and Windows: Visual QuickStart Guide by Sandee Cohen.

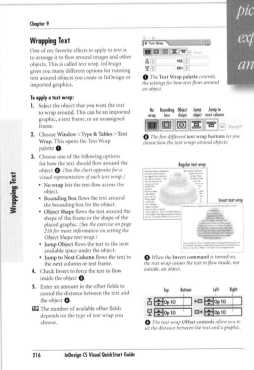

The InDesign: Visual QuickStart Guide features clear, concise, step-by-step instructions, hundreds of illustrations, and lots of helpful tips. It covers beginning to intermediate features of InDesign in detail. Take a look, and discover even more about InDesign.

1. set up document

As you probably already know, a lot is involved in creating a newsletter. Before you jump in to this project, you should have an understanding of your audience, and you should be certain that your newsletter will meet the needs of that audience. In addition, you'll need to decide certain matters of style, such as whether to use photographs, artwork, or both, what colors to use, and which typefaces will best convey your message.

In this chapter, you'll start work on a newsletter that might be produced by a parent on behalf of their child's school. You'll create the basic document, which is made up of pages, margins, columns, and a grid.

A newsletter can come in any size and format, depending on your needs and imagination. A general checklist (see extra bits on page 13) will help you determine which format is best for you.

newsletter basics

In this example project, you'll create a four-page newsletter in a standard letter size (8.5 x 11 inches) that can be folded to fit in a standard letter envelope. For this project you'll use a four-column grid.

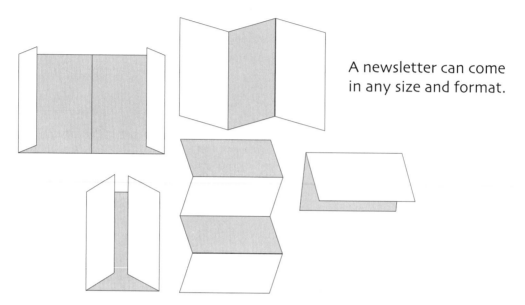

A newsletter can come in any size and format.

On the front page will be the masthead, volume number, a colored table of contents, titles, subtitles, and body text, as well as a photographic illustration. This format will be continued on the inside pages. On the upper part of the back page will be the monthly calendar; the lower portion of the back page can be used for the address panel, if you're planning to mail your newsletter.

set up document

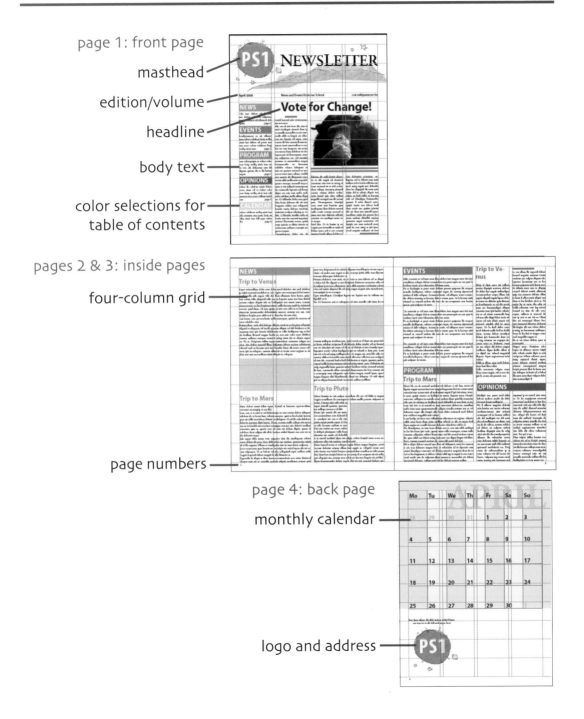

page 1: front page

masthead

edition/volume

headline

body text

color selections for table of contents

pages 2 & 3: inside pages

four-column grid

page numbers

page 4: back page

monthly calendar

logo and address

create a new document

Your four-column grid allows articles and images spanning one, two, or three columns as needed. The body text size determines the baseline grid to which to align the text in the different columns. The grid system helps to give the pages a more consistent and professional look.

1 Launch Adobe InDesign CS and choose File > New > Document (Command-N/ Ctrl-N). This grid will appear on your screen.

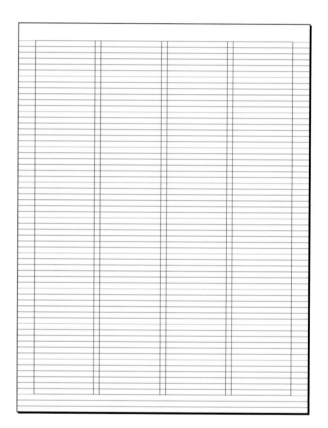

2 Set the number of pages to 4 and the number of columns to 4. Leave all the other settings at their default values and click OK.

working directory

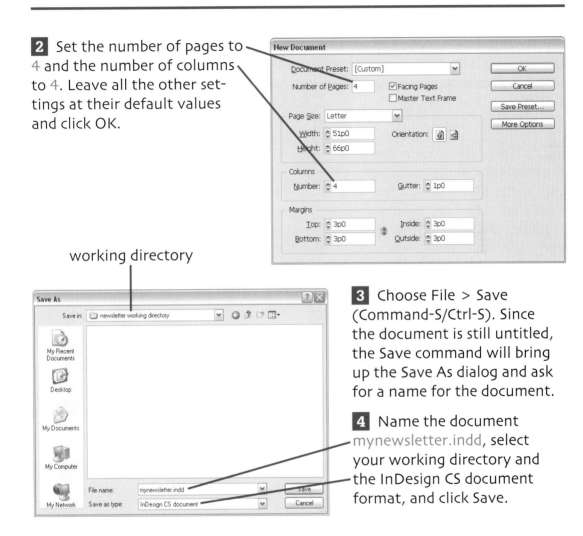

3 Choose File > Save (Command-S/Ctrl-S). Since the document is still untitled, the Save command will bring up the Save As dialog and ask for a name for the document.

4 Name the document mynewsletter.indd, select your working directory and the InDesign CS document format, and click Save.

The next time the File > Save command is invoked it will immediately save the latest changes to the specified file. The Save As dialog allows you to save your document under a new name or—as you will see later—in the InDesign CS template format.

set up document

set up baseline grid

1 To set up the baseline grid, choose Edit > Preferences > Grids in Windows or InDesign > Preferences > Grids on Macintosh.

2 In the Grids panel of the Preferences dialog, type 12 pt (12 point) in the Increment Every field. This is the default leading value of the 10 pt body text. The value in the Start field should be the same value as the top margin chosen in the New Document dialog (see previous page)—3p0 (3 picas or 36 points).

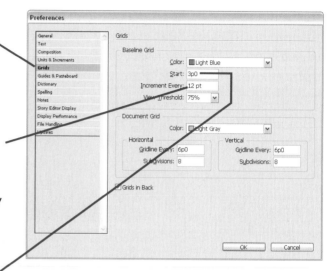

3 If you change the top margin of your document, don't forget to also change this Start position of the baseline grid. Click OK to close the Preferences dialog. Save your document.

set up document

use master pages

Elements that are used repeatedly on several, or all, pages of a document are best stored as master pages. Such elements may include grid lines, section prefix and page number placeholders, images, text, or frames ready to be used in a specific location.

You'll now set up guidelines for the placement of text and graphic frames on the page.

1 Choose Window > Pages (F12) to display the Pages palette.

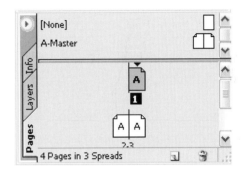

InDesign has already defined an A-Master and applied it to every page in the document; this is where the column and margin settings that you defined in the New Document dialog are stored. Modifying this A-Master will automatically modify every page in the document unless you apply a different master (or none) to a page.

2 Select the A-Master spread from the Page pop-up menu in the lower-left corner of the document window to open the spread in the document window for editing. Any change made to these pages will automatically be applied to all pages based on this master.

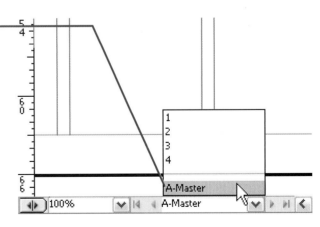

use master pages (cont.)

3 With the A-Master spread open in the document window, choose Layout > Create Guides.

4 In the Create Guides dialog, type 10 for the Number of Rows and type 0p0 in the Gutter field. You can use the columns set up in the New Document dialog as vertical guidelines, so leave the Number of Columns set at 0.

5 In the Options section of the dialog, select the Margins radio button to fit the guides to the margins.

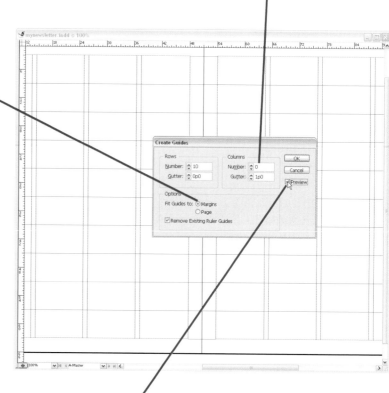

6 Check the Preview checkbox to see in the document window how these new guidelines will be placed on the spread. Click OK.

7 Save your document.

These new guidelines are now available on all document pages based on the A-Master to help position text and graphic frames.

set up document

insert page numbers

You'll now place text frames for the current page number in the lower-left and lower-right corners of the page spread. InDesign will count the pages; all you have to do is insert a special placeholder character on the master page.

You'll also see how you can simply overwrite master page elements on individual pages if necessary. You might do this, for example, if you do not want the page number to appear on the front page.

1 Choose View > Show Baseline Grid to make the baseline grid visible, if necessary. You may have to zoom in for the grid to show up.

2 Make sure View > Snap to Guides and View > Snap to Document Grid are turned on.

3 Select the Type Tool from the Toolbox. The cursor changes to a pointer inside the document window.

Type Tool (T)

insert page numbers

4 Click on the lower-left corner of the first column and drag to the right and down to create a text frame one column wide and two baselines high, then release the pointer.

Click here... ───

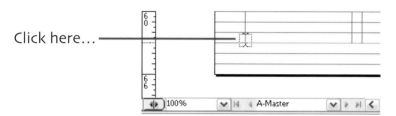

...and drag to here.

A blinking pointer will appear in the newly created text frame.

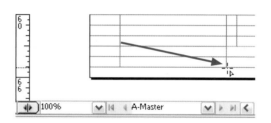

5 Choose Type > Insert Special Character > Auto Page Number (Command-Option-Shift-N/Alt-Shift-Ctrl-N). A letter A (the prefix of the master page name) will appear in the text frame, acting as a placeholder for the actual page number on the individual pages.

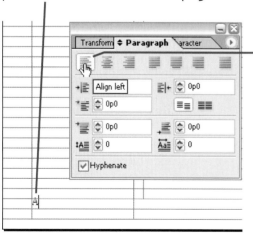

6 With the pointer still blinking in the text frame, make sure Align left is selected in the Paragraph palette.

7 Save your document.

To create the text frame for the right side of
the page, you will copy the frame you just
created on the left side and then change the
text alignment to Align right.

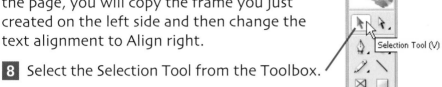

8 Select the Selection Tool from the Toolbox.

9 Click on the center of the still selected text frame, hold down the Option/
Alt key to make a copy of the frame being dragged, and start dragging to the
right. Holding down the Shift key keeps the frame at the same vertical position.

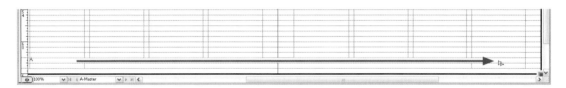

10 Drag all the way to the lower-right corner of the right side of the page
and release the pointer when the frame is vertically aligned with the far-
right column.

11 With the newly created text frame
still selected, select Align right in the
Paragraph palette.

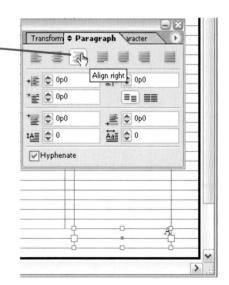

12 Save your document.

If you flip through the document pages, you
will notice the correct page number appear-
ing in the lower-left and lower-right corners
of the page. That's good enough for now.
In Chapter 3 you will apply additional text
formatting to match the design of the page
numbers to the rest of the pages.

edit page numbers

On page 1 you want to delete the page number, but you can't select the frame by clicking on it. Master page elements on a page cannot be selected for editing by simply clicking on them. This is to avoid accidental changes to elements that are supposed to be consistent on all pages.

1 Click Command-Shift/Ctrl-Shift and select the master page element on a page.

2 Go to the first page, Command-Shift/Ctrl-Shift on the text frame containing the page number to select it, and then hit the Delete key to delete it.

3 Save your document. You're done.

The page number has been deleted from the first page.

set up document

extra bits

newsletter basics p. 2

Create a checklist to help you determine the format of your newsletter.

Budget (time & money)

- Will you use color?
- How many pages will your newsletter have?
- Will it be printed on high-quality stock, on inexpensive paper, or distributed only as an email attachment?
- Will you need additional space for a sponsor notice or adver-tisement?

Target audience

- What format will best appeal to your intended readership?
- Will your newsletter be sent to most of its recipients as an email attachment?
- Is in-house printing acceptable?

Frequency and amount of information

- Will you work with an auto-mated page layout, using pre-defined templates, or will you custom design the newsletter?
- How often will you publish your newsletter—weekly, monthly, bi-monthly, annually, etc.?

- Another approach you can take when creating a newsletter is to dispense with the envelope, as in this four-page setup that features space for the address on page 4. You can save time and costs by putting the address of the recipient on the lower part of the back page and using an envelope with a window.

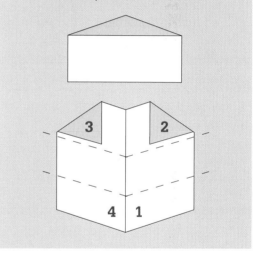

extra bits

create a new document p. 4

- InDesign's default settings—as in the New Document dialog shown on page 5—are a good starting point to get you up and running quickly. You can always change the settings for a particular document later, or set up your own default settings for all future documents. You will be presented with a four-page document, with the margins and columns set up as specified in the New Document dialog. The new document has not yet been titled or saved to disk.

set up baseline grid p. 6

- Turn on the baseline grid visibility by choosing View > Show Baseline Grid (Command-Option-`/Alt-Ctrl-`). The grid will only become visible if the current document's zoom factor is larger than the view threshold value specified in the Grid panel of the Preferences dialog. View > Hide Baseline Grid will turn off the baseline grid visibility.

use master pages p. 7

- Master pages can be based on other masters. For example, one parent master can contain elements common to all pages in the document while a child master contains only additional elements common to a subset of pages (see "Basing one master on another" in the InDesign online help).

- Remember, the guides you establish are not mandatory frame starting and ending positions for frames. But the more you can follow these guides when positioning frames on the pages, the more consistent and organized the document will look in the end.

- If you created Ruler Guides before and want to entirely replace them with new Guides, check the Remove Existing Ruler Guides checkbox. Leave it unchecked if you want to create additional guides.

set up document

2. work with text frames

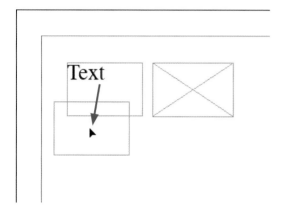

InDesign's frames are containers for text and graphics. In this chapter, you will create the frames for your text, link the frames together, and fill them with placeholder copy. You'll also create a placeholder frame for the graphic. Both text frames and graphic frames can be moved or otherwise altered to adjust the layout of the newsletter.

Although you'll use placeholder text for this project, you can easily enter text by importing it from a word processing application (using the copy and paste functions), or by typing directly in InDesign.

create a text frame

You'll create one text frame in the left column of page 1 for a table of contents and a second text frame spanning columns 2–4 next to the table of contents. At the top of the page, leave space for a masthead which you'll add later.

1 Open the mynewsletter. indd document created in Chapter 1.

In the Pages palette, double-click on the icon for page 1 to open page 1 in the document window. If the Pages palette is not visible, choose Window > Pages (or click the F12 function key) to show the Pages palette.

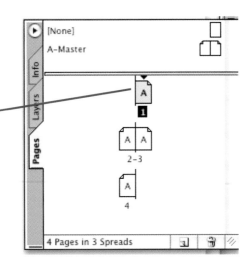

2 Select the Type Tool from the Toolbox.

work with text frames

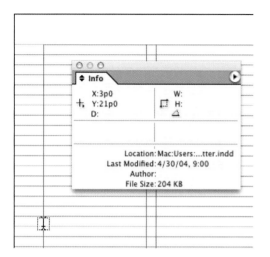

3 Make sure that the Info palette is visible (Window > Info or press F8), and that Snap to Guides and Snap to Document Grid are turned on (View > Snap to Guides, View > Snap to Document Grid).

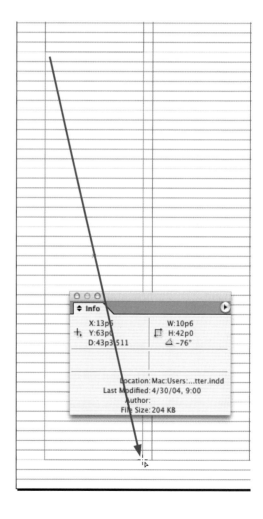

4 Move the cursor to the left side of the first column, about one third of the page down from the top. Look at the Info palette and move the pointer until you are exactly 3 picas from the left edge of the page and 21 picas from the top edge of the page.

5 Click and drag with the pointer to the lower-right corner of column 1. Release the pointer when the Info palette indicates a frame width of 10p6 and a height of 42p.

You now have a text frame the width of one column and the height of seven guide rows. An insertion point (the I-beam shape) is blinking in the top-left corner of the frame, ready to fill the frame with text.

work with text frames

add placeholder text

You can either type your copy in the text frame or, as you'll do here, make use of a great InDesign feature: placeholder text—dummy copy that can later be easily replaced with your final text.

With the insertion point still blinking in the newly created text frame, choose Type > Fill with Placeholder Text, and the text frame will fill with the text. You will learn to format the text in Chapter 3.

Ci bla feugiam, vel ulputem nit vel iriurem doloree tueraessit ad tat nit at.
Mod magnit, commy num zzrit lut volobor suscili andipsum niat. Utpat, core tin hendreriure modit alit ero dolore facin veniam, core commodig- uibh eriureet, vuilam, veliscipsum nis at. Secte tem dunt nosto od ex et iusto estie mod eum vent nostin ex eugait vullam ing ero conse conse tis nulput prat. Ut lum nim am ver adiam et, sit alisit dolor susciliquam ilisis- sismod dolorero etuer am, sum iusto consent dolore dolenit praessent iliquat. Ex erci tat. Obore corem erat at iuscipit, sequis et eugiam, sequat praessissi bla commodipit praesed tat.
Et iuscincip er sustion sendio conse tem venim ing ex et autpatum ipis et, commy nonum nullandit ute facidunt nis nonul- luptat, qui bla con verci bla consectem volor iril dolorpe raestrud eumsan

make second frame

With the Type Tool still selected, create a second text frame by clicking anywhere in column 2 and dragging about an inch to the right and down. Don't worry about the exact position and dimensions of the text frame; you will fix that on the next page.

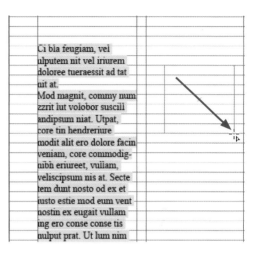

position the text frame

1 Choose the Selection Tool from the Toolbox. The selected frame has eight handles (one in each corner and one in the middle of each side) to resize the frame, plus two in and out ports which are discussed later in this chapter.

2 Click inside the frame (not on any of the eight handles) and drag the frame next to the frame in column 1. The frame snaps into position when the top-left corner of the frame is close to the left side of column 2 and the guideline is 21p from the top of the page. Release the pointer.

Ci bia feugiam, vel ulputem nit vel iriurem doloree tueraessit ad tat nit at.
Mod magnit, commy num zzrit iut volobor suscili andipsum niat. Utpat, core tin hendreriure modit alit ero dolore facin veniam, core commodig- nibh eriureet, vullam, veliscipsum nis at. Secte tem dunt nosto od ex et iusto estie mod eum vent nostin ex eugait vullam ing ero conse conse tis nulput prat. Ut lum nim

work with text frames

3 Click on the lower-right handle of the text frame and drag to the lower-right corner of the last column on the page. Again, the frame snaps to the column and guidelines when you get close enough to them.

add placeholder text

With the text frame still selected, choose Type > Fill with Placeholder Text. Note that you don't have to switch to the Type Tool first to be able to select this option.

Ci bla feugiam, vel ulputem nit vel iriurem doloree tueraessit ad tat nit at.
Mod magnit, commy num zzrit lut volobor suscili andipsum niat. Utpat, core tin hendreriure modit alit ero dolore facin veniam, core commodignibh eriureet, vullam, veliscipsum nis at. Secte tem dunt nosto od ex et iusto estie mod eum vent nostin ex eugait vullam ing ero conse conse tis nulput prat. Ut lum nim am ver adiam et, sit alisit dolor susciliquam ilisissismod dolorero etuer am, sum iusto consent dolore dolenit praessent iliquat. Ex erci tat. Obore corem erat at iuscipit, sequis et eugiam, sequat praessissi bla commodipit praesed tat.
Et iuscincip er sustion sendio conse tem venim ing ex et autpatum ipis et, commy nonum nullandit ute facidunt nis nonulluptat, qui bla con verci bla consectem volor iril dolorpe raestrud eumsan

Accum ver susci tetum dolor sum zzril iurem do odo dit venim vercillummod dolesto euismol orerate magna feu feu feugue estis nostinim aliscipsummy nim aliquam in exer am, consequ ationsed deliqui smoloreet, consenim inibh eu feuguer in ea ad magna ad tat nulluptat vel dunt lutpatuer ationsed exerit, vullandre modit ver amcorem veraessit vulla faccum digna conullum volore do ea faci te do endit num alit lum dolore min exercillamet venisism nit lore tio ea conum iurercipsum vullandre dolorem zzriliq natetue diamet nonsectet ut nis et, vendiam consequ iscing ea faccum nullumsan henisi.
Ectem num vent vel dolenim ex exeril iliqui estrud tiorsent pratinit at ing er inim digna feugait ate faccum quate tatie magnibh endre commy nullandigna consequ ismodolore tatis nis dolorero delendr enustrud tatuer at augiatum nim el dui tin venis autatum zzriure feu faci blaore magnit nos nim quating eugait, si.
Uscip et, se modipit lor suscipsummy nonum adiamet ummodolorper ad ercin veliqui scidunt lummy nullam iustin et lut aliquat. Ut num quis dolor ilit nit wisismo loreet aut lore doluptat prat alisi euis nulputpatie ming enim quissis non erit dionsendipis do dit esse etuercidunt alisl ipsum init auguero iliquat lortis dunt ad tat. Ut accum duismodip el irilla facilis alit at. Amet exer suscidus doluptatum quisit amet lum autatue modo dip exeriustrud exero consent inci te mincin utpat.
Putatum dolessequam irit utpat num nibh ex estrud modolor sis nostrud modolenim ad molorem ipis adion utpatum nulput lore mod mod magna consenit atem eum nullam ipit nullum vendrem del ute consed delis dit acip enim vullut nulput alit alis ese cortisim ipit acilla feu feum alit eugait augiatue eliquatie modignibh et eum quam zzril elit at. Utat ut wis augiat.
Sim illamco rpercilit dio ex euisism veliquat.
Ullut la feuguer sequisi tatumsandiam velis erciniatis aciduipit essi tismolo bortion sequisi blaorerat, qui ex esequisim del ea coreriurer secte modnt veriureet lorem zzrilit lortisl incing eniat vercidu ipisis amconsendit nulla consecte diam, susto consequipit praestin velisl ipisis eum do odolessendre dunt alit, quat accumsan hendre dio ea faccum quat volore feugiat ionullan ullam, ver si.
It wis dion essi. Giam qui et incinisit ipsummy nit nonsequat.
Facing eum quat wisi tet alis do consecte ex esed min et ullan henismo dionsequis augue digna feum ipsum zzriurem velis nonsed modo esed tisisl delit loreet niametuerit, conse ercincin velent nostrud te vel ea aliquat, quisit ad magna acil ulla facip eugue consed ea commolor il utat. Ut lortin et nostionsed essis ex ex eseniamet praese modolore do odiamcore doleseq uisisis dit adigna facilla faccum vulla

set column number

1 With the frame selected, choose Object > Text Frame Options (Command-B/Alt-B). Set the number of columns to 3 and the gutter width to 1p0, the same gutter width as specified in the New Document dialog.

2 Turn on the Preview option to see the effect of your selection in the background.

3 Click OK. Save your document.

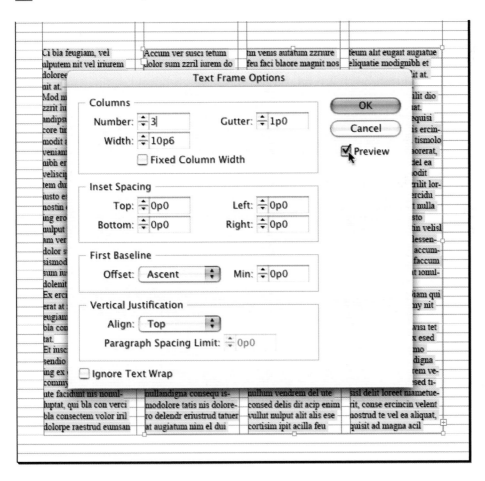

create graphic frame

Now you'll create a placeholder frame for a graphic inside this text frame.

Select the Rectangle Frame tool from the Toolbox and draw a rectangle inside the large text frame spanning the two right columns of the document. Make the rectangle about two inches high.

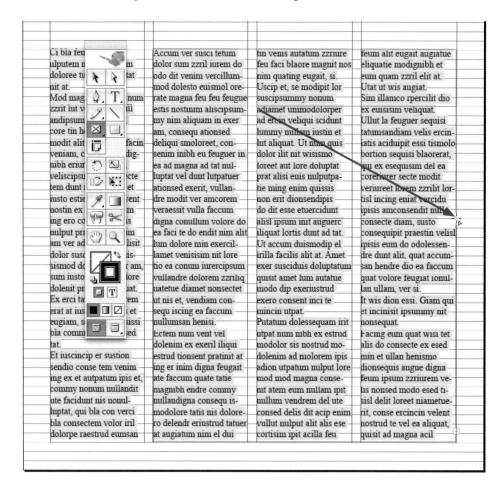

wrap text

The text frame's placeholder text needs to wrap around the graphic frame.

With the graphic frame selected, choose Wrap around bounding box in the Text Wrap palette (Window > Type & Tables > Text Wrap).

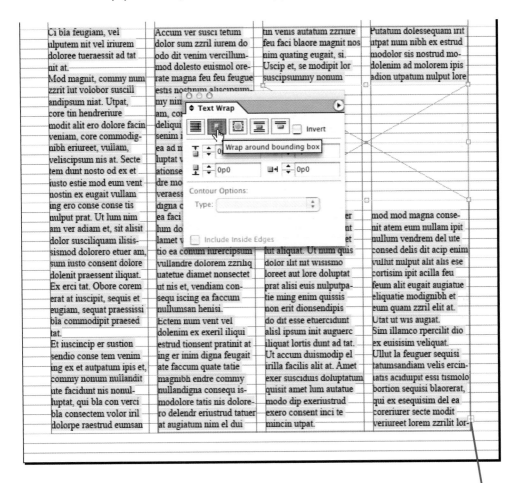

The text underneath now wraps around the placeholder graphic frame, and the out port on the lower-right side of the text frame now contains a red plus sign indicating that more text is loaded in this frame than can be displayed: You created a text overflow.

link text frames

Now create a text frame on page 3 to hold the text that can no longer fit on page 1.

1 Select the Selection Tool and click on the red plus sign in the lower-right corner of the large text frame on page 1. The pointer will change to a loaded text icon.

2 Double-click on the page 3 icon in the Pages palette.

3 Click with the loaded text icon in the right-most column on page 3 close to the top margin of the page. InDesign will create a new frame in the right column of the page (snapping to column grid and guides) large enough to hold the additional text overflowing from page 1.

work with text frames

The two text frames are now linked. If a change on page 1 results in more or less text fitting in the frame on page 1, the frame on page 3 will automatically update to contain the remaining text of the story. You can visualize the link between the two frames by choosing View > Show Text Threads.

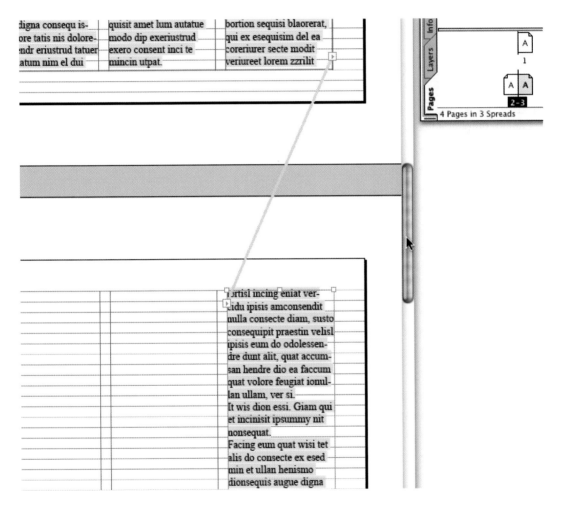

use the story editor

With InDesign, you edit text either in the Layout view or in the Story Editor. The Story Editor lets you concentrate on the content of the story, with the actual layout of the text carried out in the background. This lets you type faster with less distraction. The left column in the Story Editor displays formatting information associated with each paragraph, while the right column contains the actual text.

1 With the text frame selected, choose Edit > Edit in Story Editor (Ctrl-Y/Command-Y).

2 To close the Story Editor window, choose Edit > Edit in Layout.

3 Save your document.

Story Editor

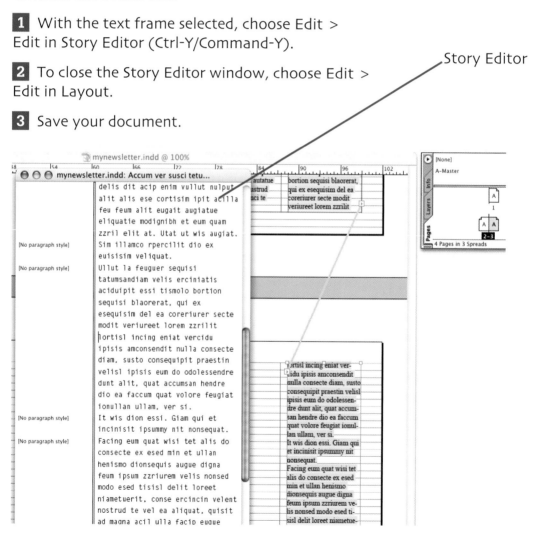

work with text frames

add "continued" text

So that your newsletter readers will know on which page the story continues, create a "continued on page xy" text frame at the end of the text frame on page 1. InDesign knows on which page to find the linked text frame and can automatically insert the correct page number. You'll need to create a text frame overlapping, or at least touching, the text frame on page 1, and insert a special character that InDesign will replace with the correct page number.

1 Choose Edit > Deselect All (Command-Shift-A/ Ctrl-Shift-A).

2 Select the Text Tool and create a small text frame under the last column on page 1. To avoid selecting the text within the existing frame, click outside the text frame (about one line below the last line of text) and drag to the right and upwards (overlapping the existing text frame) to create the new frame.

add "continued" text

3 With the Selection Tool and the new frame selected, choose Wrap around bounding box from the Text Wrap palette. Any text pushed out of the large text frame on page 1 automatically reflows into the linked frame on page 3.

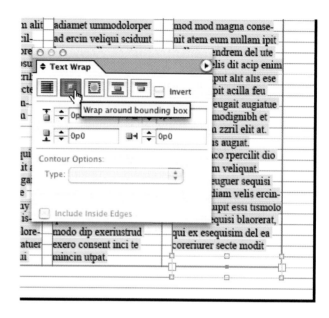

4 Select the Text Tool and click in the newly created text frame (or simply double-click the text frame with the Selection Tool). Type continued on page (with a space after "page"), then choose Type > Insert Special Character > Next Page Number. InDesign will insert the page number for you. If you move the frame on page 3 to a different page, InDesign will update the reference on page 1.

5 Save your document.

work with text frames

create headline

Create a big headline spanning the three columns of the large text frame on the right. The number of columns is defined on a per-text-frame basis. That means you will need a separate text frame just for the headline if you want it to span the three columns of the main story. To make a place for the headline text frame, move the top border of the main text frame down a little.

1 Open the mynewsletter.indd document you worked on in Chapter 2.

2 Navigate to page 1.

3 Choose the Selection Tool from the Toolbox and click inside the three-column text frame to select it.

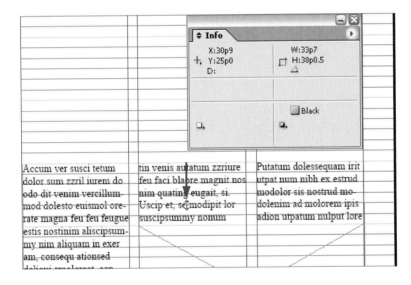

4 Grab the center top handle of the frame and move it down by 4 picas. For precise movement you can use the Info palette (F8) or turn on the baseline grid (View > Show Baseline Grid). One baseline height is 1 pica in your document, so move the top of the frame down by four baselines.

create headline

5 Select the Type Tool and create a new text frame from position X:14p6, Y:21p0 to position X:48p0, Y:25p0.

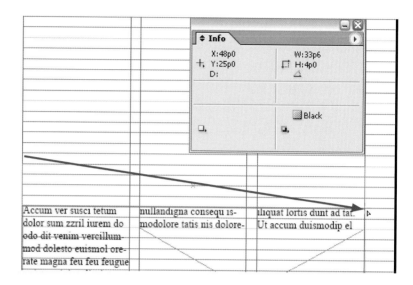

6 With the cursor blinking in the newly created text frame, type Vote for Change!

7 Select all the text in that text frame (Command-A/Ctrl-A).

8 In the Control palette (Command-Option-6/Alt-Ctrl-6), select Myriad Pro from the Font Family menu and then Bold from the Type Style menu. Set the Font Size to 48pt.

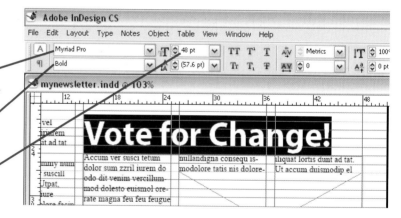

creating and applying styles

align headline

With the text still selected, select Align center from the Paragraph palette (Window > Type & Tables > Paragraph).

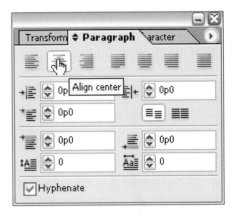

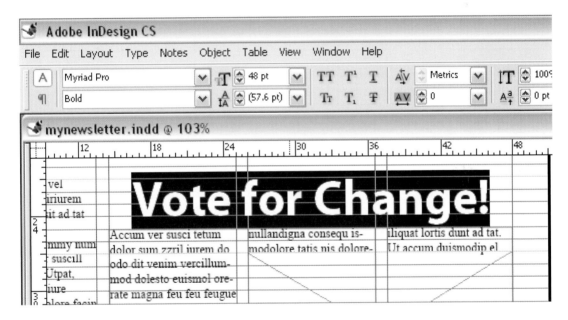

format body text

1 Select the Type Tool and click anywhere in the text of the main story.

2 Choose Edit > Select All (Command-A/Ctrl-A). This will select all text in the story including the text in the additional text frame on page 3.

3 Open the Character palette (Window > Type & Tables > Character) and select Adobe Garamond Pro Regular 10pt.

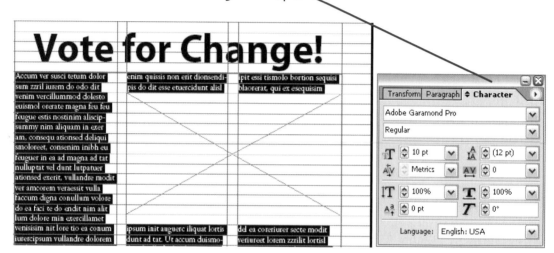

creating and applying styles

align and justify text

1 To make sure body text in adjacent columns lines up horizontally, open the Paragraph palette and select Align to Baseline Grid.

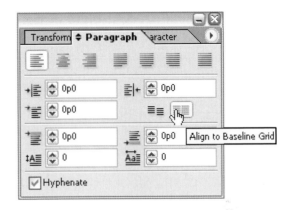

2 Select Justify with last line aligned left from the Paragraph palette.

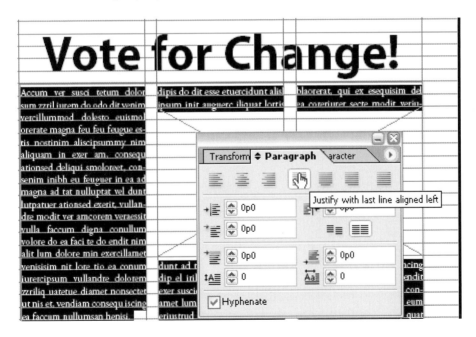

add byline

Now you'll add a byline—the name of the author set in a different typeface—at the beginning of the story.

1 Click just in front of the first character of the story. You should see a blinking pointer in the top-left corner of the text frame.

If you click too far to the left (outside of the text frame), normally no harm is done. If you click and drag and accidentally create a new text frame, it's always good to know that InDesign can undo your last step (or even multiple steps). If you undo too many steps, it lets you redo them (check out Edit > Undo [name of last command]; Command-Z/Ctrl-Z, and Edit > Redo [name of previously undone command]; Shift-Command-Z/ Shift-Ctrl-Z).

2 Type By John Thomsen and press Return.

creating and applying styles

format byline

1 Select the byline by triple-clicking on it.

2 Choose Adobe Garamond Pro Italic 9pt in the Control or Character palette.

3 Select Align center from the Paragraph palette.

4 Select Do Not Align to Baseline Grid in the Paragraph palette.

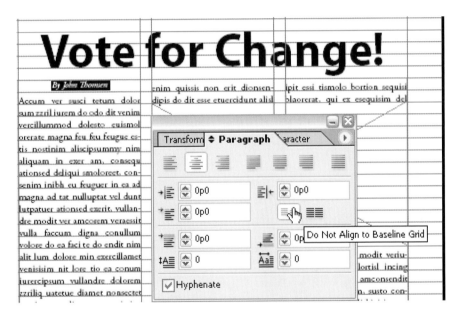

5 If you haven't done so recently, save your document.

create caption

The picture (for now you only have the empty placeholder frame) should be aligned with the top of the main story frame. You'll add another text frame underneath to hold the caption text.

1 Choose the Selection Tool from the Toolbox and click on the placeholder frame for your picture to select it. Move the center-top handle up to a Y position of 25 picas.

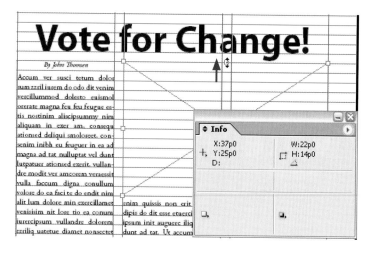

2 Select the Type Tool from the Toolbox, click in the margin area next to the lower-right corner of the picture frame, and drag to create a frame about two lines high and two columns wide.

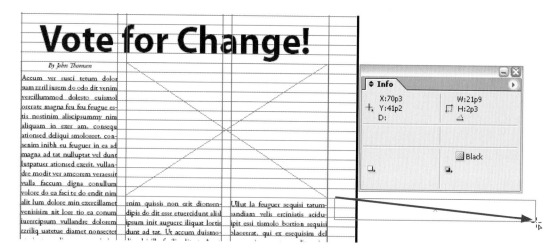

creating and applying styles

make second frame

Create one more text frame between where you'll place the masthead and the beginning of the articles. This line of text will hold the date, Web address, and volume number.

1 Scroll to the upper third of page 1.

2 With the Type Tool, create a text frame four columns wide and about two baselines high—from position X:3p0, Y:18p6 to position X:48p0, Y:20p8.

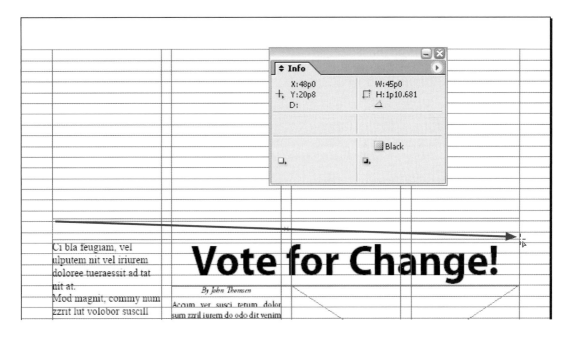

format text frame

1 Select Justify all lines and Do Not Align to Baseline Grid in the Paragraph palette.

2 Select Myriad Pro Regular 12pt in the Control palette.

3 Type April 2005 (don't worry about the strange character spacing while you're typing), then choose Type > Insert White Space > Flush Space.

4 Type http://www.publicschoolone.org/newsletter and again choose Type > Insert White Space > Flush Space, then type Volume 8.

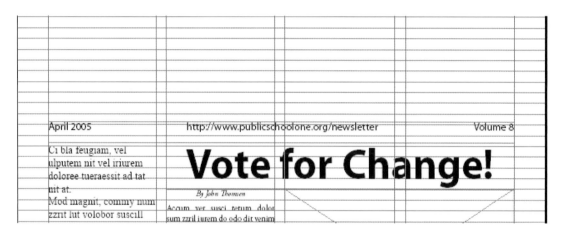

5 Save your document.

create body style

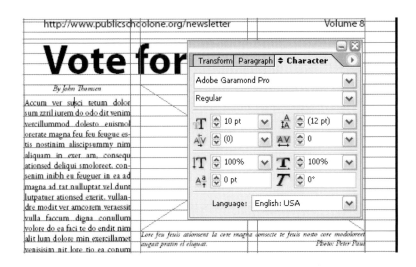

1 With the Type Tool, click anywhere in the first paragraph of the main three-column story, but at least one line below the byline. Confirm that the Character palette (and the Control palette) reads Adobe Garamond Pro Regular at 10 points.

2 Open the Paragraph Styles palette (Window > Type & Tables > Paragraph Styles or F11). It reads [No paragraph style] at the top. Click on the triangle next to it and select New Paragraph Style from the menu.

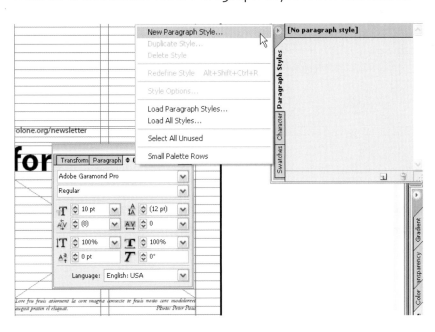

The New Paragraph Style dialog opens up to show formatting settings of the current paragraph. In this project, you will only deal with some of the Basic Character Formats.

create body style (cont.)

3 Click on Basic Character Formats in the list on the left and confirm that it is displaying the formatting you applied to your body text. In the Style Name field, name this style Body and click OK.

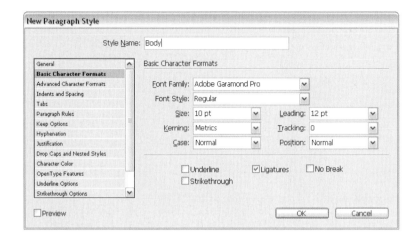

The name Body will now appear in the list of Paragraph Styles in the Paragraph Styles palette. Note that [No paragraph style] is selected. You only defined a new paragraph style based on the formatting of the paragraph the pointer is in, but you did not yet assign this style to the current paragraph.

creating and applying styles

assign body style

1 Press Shift-Command-End/Shift-Ctrl-End to select all the text/paragraphs to the end of the story. Note that the text on page 3 is also selected, but the byline (which has a different formatting applied) is not selected.

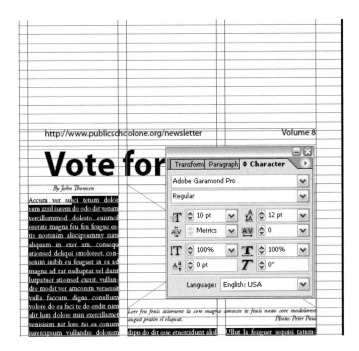

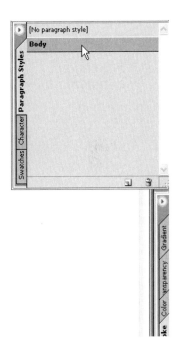

assign body style (cont.)

2 Now click on Body in the Paragraph Styles palette to assign this style to all the selected paragraphs.

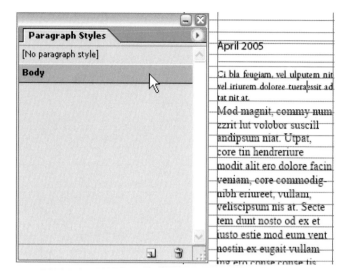

3 Select the text in column 1 (Edit > Select All or Command-A/Ctrl-A) and click again on Body in the Paragraph Styles palette. With a single click you've just assigned your preferred formatting for body text to all the paragraphs in the story.

4 Save your document.

creating and applying styles

create byline style

1 Click anywhere in the byline of the main story. Choose New Paragraph Style in the Paragraph Styles palette, name the style Byline, and click OK.

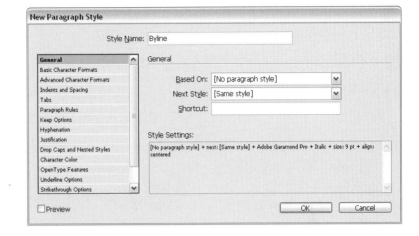

2 With the cursor still blinking in the byline, apply the Byline paragraph style by selecting Byline from the Paragraph Styles palette.

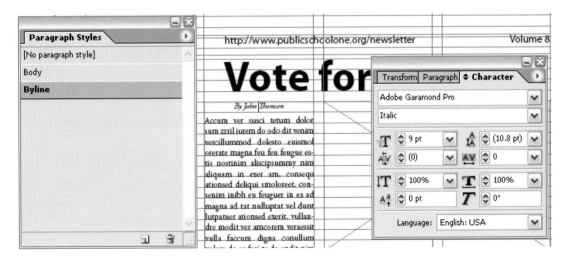

create caption style

1 Click in the caption text under the picture placeholder frame. Define a new paragraph style and call it Caption.

2 Assign this Caption style to the caption text.

3 Select the text Photo: Peter Paul at the end of this paragraph and select Regular from the Type Style menu in the Character palette.

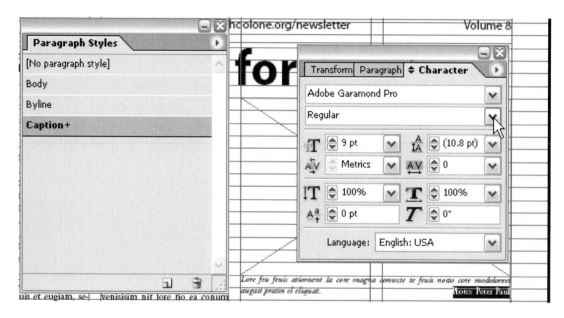

In step 3, you changed the formatting (overwritten the paragraph style) of some text within the paragraph, just as you would, for example, change one word to italic in the body text. Note the plus sign at the end of the word Caption in the Paragraph Styles palette, indicating that some additional formatting has been applied to part or all of the paragraph.

add large head style

Click on the large headline on page 1. Define a new paragraph style, call it Head large, and apply that style to the large headline.

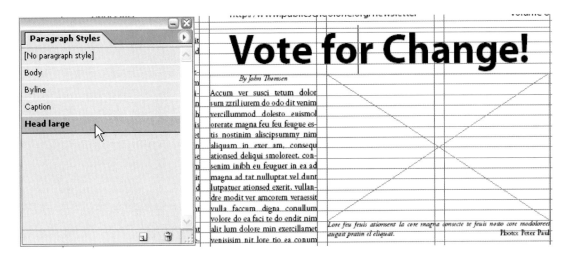

add medium head

You can create a new style based on a previously defined style. That's what you'll do now to define a medium headline, based on the settings for the large headline style. We will use the medium headline style for the table of contents headings in Chapter 4.

1 Choose Edit > Deselect All (Shift-Command-A/Shift-Ctrl-A).

2 Choose New Paragraph Style from the menu in the Paragraph Styles palette.

3 Call the new style Head medium and choose Based On: Head large in the General panel of the dialog.

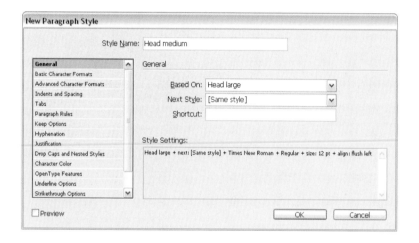

4 Now click on Basic Character Formats in the list on the left and change the point size to 24 point.

5 Click OK.

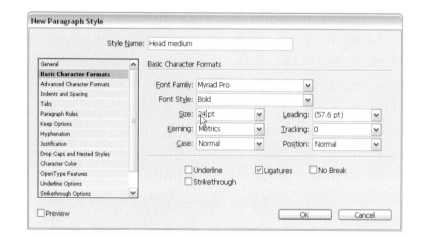

creating and applying styles

add small head style

1 Create one last paragraph style based on Head large, call it Head small and give it a size of 12 points.

2 With the Text Tool, click on the line containing the date, Web page address, and volume number. Apply the Head small paragraph style by clicking on Head small in the Paragraph Styles palette.

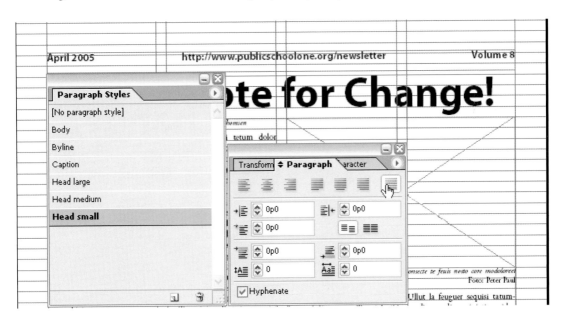

justify small headline

1 Now reapply the Justify all lines setting in the Paragraph palette. In general, we want the small headlines to be centered like the large headlines. You would use small headlines at the start of a new section within a long story. In this case, though, we apply additional formatting to the paragraph to spread the text to the full page width. Note the plus sign after Head small in the Paragraph Styles palette. The Justify all lines setting overwrites the default settings in this paragraph.

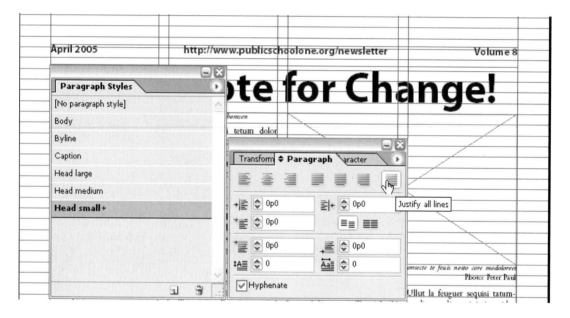

2 Save your document.

extra bits

font overview p. 34

- Clear, legible, inviting typography will compel people to read your newsletter. Bad typography will have the opposite effect. Your selection of typefaces creates a mood. Choosing the right font for your newsletter is not easy, as there are thousands of fonts all designed to fit different needs. And the quality of the typefaces is not equal. Well-established type foundries like Adobe, Berthold, ITC, and Linotype set a high standard for creating their digital fonts. On the other hand, the free fonts found on the Web are often not well designed and have poor quality when it comes to equal space distribution or printing. In addition, the free fonts frequently don't come with an extended character set or are only available in a single style. Technically imperfect fonts can wreak havoc on your computer or at your service bureau. With fonts, you get what you pay for.

- One good way to check out different combinations of typefaces is to go to www.adobe.com/type. There the different fonts are categorized by use, style, classification, and theme. There is even a list of recommended fonts to be used in a newsletter!

a checklist for selecting typefaces

- Is the font for the body text easy to read both in print and on the Web?

- Does the headline font have visual impact and complement the body text font?

- Does the font family, especially for the body text, come in a range of weights and widths?

extra bits

create headline p. 35

- In general, defining a visual system helps to organize the information in a consistent way. However, there is no need to slavishly follow your guidelines. If there is a need for a certain headline to stand out more than the others, or to fill a certain amount of space, you can play with the point size or kerning and tracking settings to adjust the size and spacing of your headline—just don't do it so often that your system is no longer apparent.

- Keep things simple: Don't mix too many type styles, colors, and sizes. To accomplish a contrast between two styles, it is often enough to change just one characteristic of the font, such as changing the point size or using bold instead of regular. There's absolutely no need to use italics, boldface, and an underline to give a word emphasis.

- When typing text, the context-sensitive Control palette (Window > Control) gives you quick access to the settings otherwise entered through the Character palette (Window > Type & Tables > Character; Command-T/Ctrl-T).

- See "Turning Pages" in the InDesign online help for the many ways you can navigate through your document.

align headline p. 37

- Use the Paragraph palette to change the justification settings for the paragraph.

align and justify text p. 39

- InDesign does a superb job of justifying text. By default, it uses the Adobe Paragraph Composer, which calculates the best line-break positions for an entire paragraph to yield the best overall result.

format byline p. 41

- In general, you'll only want to align the body text to the baseline grid. Lines or paragraphs with a different point size—like bylines or sub-headlines—should be freely floating within the body text, which is tagged to the baseline grid.

creating and applying styles

create caption p. 42

- To create the text frame for the caption, it is easiest to first create the text frame on the right margin of the document and then move it into position.

- As with the byline text, the caption text should not be aligned with the baseline grid, since it has a different point size than the body text. Once the actual picture is in place, you will probably have to move the text frame down a little to add space between the picture and the caption.

create body style p. 49

- The two icons (page and trashcan) in the lower-right corner of the Paragraph Styles palette are shortcuts to two menu items: New Paragraph Style and Delete Style.

- A paragraph is selected even if only a few characters of the paragraph are part of the current text selection. A single paragraph is also selected if the blinking pointer is located somewhere within that paragraph.

add medium head p. 56

- You only need to change those aspects of the paragraph style that you want to be different from the original; all the other settings of the paragraph are inherited from the original paragraph style.

creating and applying styles 61

4. add lines and color

Now that you've set up the basic type styles for your newsletter, you can think about additional graphic treatments to make your story more visually compelling. These can range from minor changes of the graphic style—such as adding a line, a frame, or colored text—to including an illustration or a photo. These graphic devices can strengthen the visual impact and mood you want to project. On the other hand, meaningless graphic flourishes can clutter your message—less is more! In graphics, as in writing, using emphasis too frequently diminishes its power. In the case of your newsletter, the color scheme used for the graphic devices relates to the masthead graphics, which conveys a more unified look.

what you'll do

In this chapter, you will draw two lines to visually separate the masthead from the articles, and create colored background frames for the table of contents, which will establish color codes for the different sections of the newsletter.

lines ——

color frames for —— table of contents

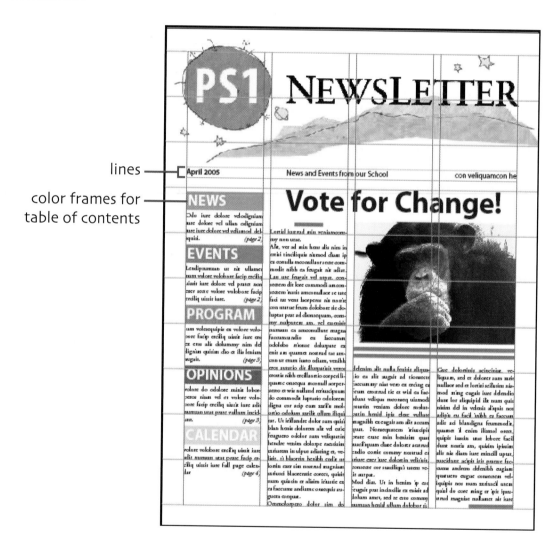

create a line

1 Open the mynewsletter.indd document.

2 Select the Line Tool from the Toolbox.

3 Make sure that View > Snap to Guides and View > Snap to Document Grid are still turned on.

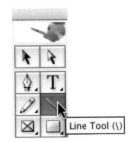

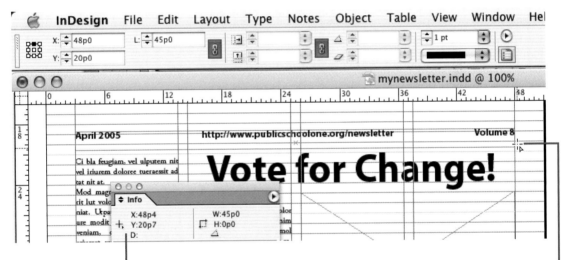

4 Use the Info palette to help you position the pointer at X:3p0 and Y:20p0, then click and start dragging to the right. While dragging, hold down the Shift key to constrain the line to a 45-degree angle (you want a perfectly horizontal line). Once the pointer is located close to position X:48p0, Y:20p0, release it, then release the Shift key.

create a line (cont.)

5 With the line still selected, you can change some of its attributes in the Control palette. Click on the line width pop-up menu and change the line width to 0.5 pt.

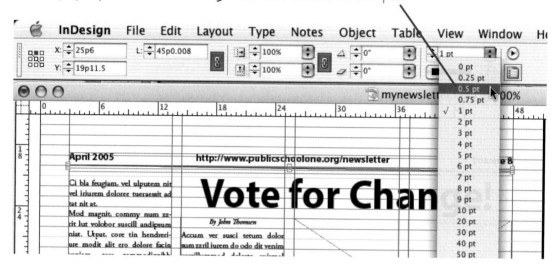

add lines and color

copy line

To make a second, identical line with only a change in the position, the Step and Repeat dialog enables you to quickly create and precisely position one or more copies of an object.

1 With the line selected, choose Edit > Step and Repeat (Command-Shift-V/Ctrl-Shift-V). (If you have no object selected, the Step and Repeat command is dimmed.)

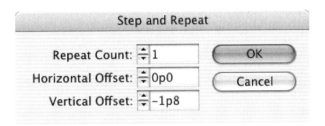

2 Enter 1 for the Repeat Count, 0 for the Horizontal Offset, and -1p8 for Vertical Offset, then click OK. If you are not satisfied with the position of the new line, nudge it up or down using the arrow keys.

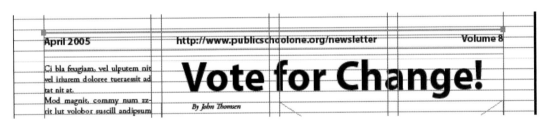

3 Save your document.

create color swatches

A clear color code organizes your content to help readers quickly recognize the different sections of your newsletter. Here, you'll create colorful headlines for the table of contents on the left side of page 1. First, define color swatches for the newsletter's five sections.

A monochromatic color system made of tints of one color nicely ties together extremely different graphic devices and illustrations.

1 Select New Color Swatch from the menu in the Swatches palette (Window > Swatches or F5).

2 Deselect Name with Color Value and name this new swatch news orange. Select Process as Color Type and CMYK as Color Mode, then set the color to Cyan (C): 0%, Magenta (M): 75%, Yellow (Y): 95%, Black (K): 0%. Click OK.

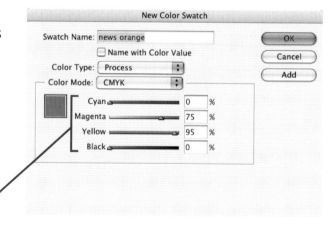

add lines and color

3 Create four more swatches: events blue with C=95, M=5, Y=25, K=0; program green with C=85, M=0, Y=100, K=0; opinions purple with C=65, M=90, Y=15, K=5; and calendar yellow with C=0, M=25, Y=95, K=0.

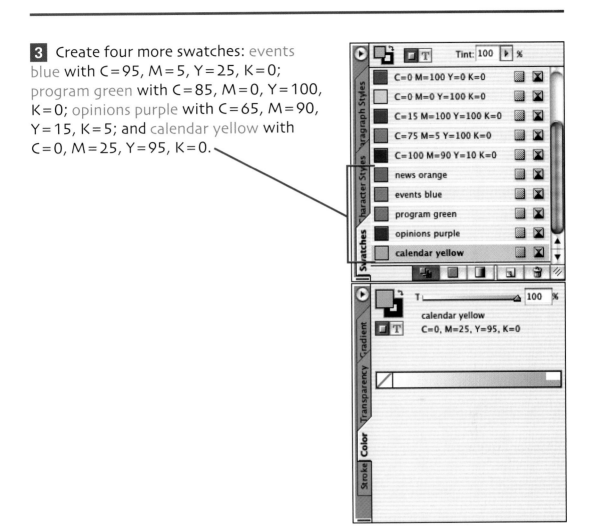

create a color head

Here you'll create a frame containing the headline text, change the background color of that frame, and paste it inside the table of contents text stream. That way you will get one line of text with a different background color.

Use the white space to the left of page 1 to prepare the frame with the headline.

1 Use the Type Tool to create a text frame—one column wide and two-and-a-half baseline grids high—in the white area to the left of page 1.

2 Select the Selection Tool. The newly created frame should now be selected.

3 The Control palette, which is docked to the top of the document window and displays different options depending on the type of object selected, features the Constrain Proportions icon. Deselect this when resizing the frame—the icon will display a broken chain.

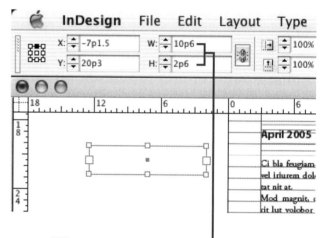

4 Set the width to 10p6 and the height to 2p6.

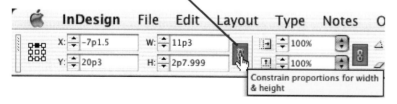

5. images and tables

When you're working with photos and illustrations, it's beneficial to use a consistent style or a combination of complementary styles that achieves a professional look. You could, for example, convert all your photos to black-and-white, which will not only reduce the cost of printing, but also visually tie the images together.

In this chapter, you'll place the masthead image and a photo on page 1 of the document, positioning and adjusting the images to fit into the allocated space. You'll also create a calendar page on the back of the newsletter using InDesign's sophisticated Table tool.

When presenting tables, don't just use the default design—try to match its style to the look and feel of the other illustrations in your document. InDesign offers a large set of very powerful tools that makes the task of designing and formatting tables easy.

place a prepared image

You will need an image to function as the masthead for your newsletter. The area reserved for the masthead is about 8.5 by 3 inches. When printed, the image should have at least a resolution of about 250 dpi. Therefore you need to create an image—text, picture, drawing—of roughly 2100 x 750 pixels. Before following the steps in this chapter, prepare a picture with similar specifications in the image-editing or drawing application of your choice.

1 Open the mynewsletter.indd document.

2 Navigate to the top of page 1.

3 Make sure nothing is selected (choose Edit > Deselect All if this menu item is not dimmed already).

4 Choose File > Place (Command-D/Ctrl-D). In the Place dialog, select and open the prepared masthead file, e.g., a Photoshop file.

5 The pointer will change to a loaded graphics icon. Click in the top-left corner of the page, just inside the page. InDesign will create a graphic frame and place the picture inside it.

Click here with the loaded graphics icon and InDesign will place the image at the top of the page.

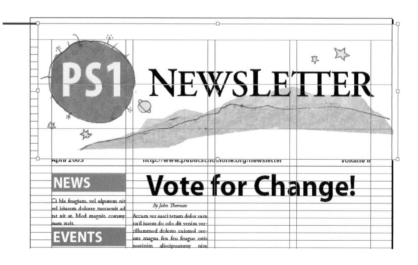

position the image

The placed image is about the right size, but still needs to be positioned. Also, since part of the picture is hiding the text on the page, you need to move the picture behind the other objects on the page.

1 With the newly created graphic frame selected, choose Object > Arrange > Send to Back (Shift-Command-[/Shift-Ctrl-[). The text and other objects on the page will no longer be hidden behind the picture.

2 With the Selection Tool, click on the selected frame and drag the picture to its final position. You can also use the arrow keys to nudge the picture into place.

3 Save your document.

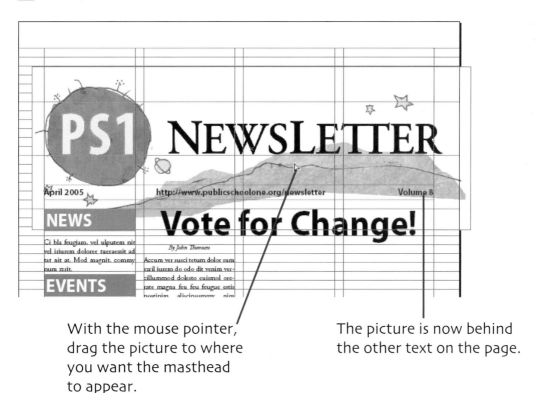

With the mouse pointer, drag the picture to where you want the masthead to appear.

The picture is now behind the other text on the page.

resize an image

Now you'll deal with the more common situation: a photo that needs to be resized in InDesign.

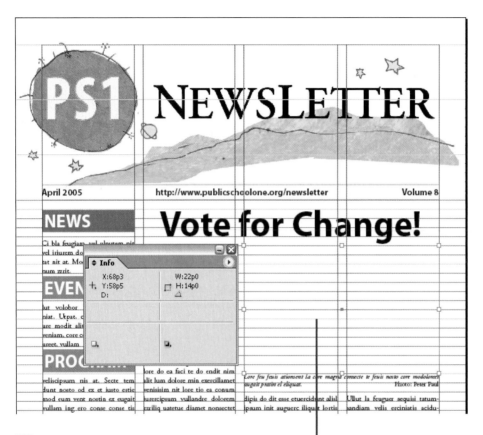

1 With the Selection Tool, click on the graphic frame inside the main story frame to select it.

2 Choose File > Place and select a photo taken with your digital camera, usually in jpeg format, with a resolution of at least 1000 x 600 pixels. Most digital cameras (and Photoshop) assign a default value of 72 dpi when saving jpeg files. This means that the picture is much too large when first loaded into its graphic frame.

3 To see the entire photo within its graphic frame, select the frame with the Selection Tool and choose Object > Fitting > Fit Content Proportionally.

enlarge and crop

It turns out that the aspect ratio (width to height) of the picture is not the same as the aspect ratio of the graphic frame. The photo is too narrow when fitted to the exact height of the graphic frame. Here, you'll enlarge the picture to fill the width of the frame and then crop part of the image on the top and/or bottom.

1 Select the Direct Selection Tool from the Toolbox.

2 Click on the picture within the graphic frame.

When you need to select an object that is part of a larger object (such as in this situation, where you want to select the actual picture within the picture frame), use the Direct Selection Tool.

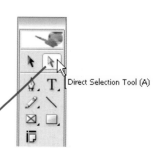

Direct Selection Tool (A)

Vote for Change!

By John Thomsen

Accum ver susci tetum dolor sum zzril iurem do odo dit venim vercillummod dolesto euismol orerate magna feu feu feugue estis nostinim aliscipsummy nim aliquam in exer am, consequ ationsed deliqui smoloreet, consenim inibh eu feuguer in ea ad magna ad tat nulluptat vel dunt lutpatuer ationsed exerit, vullandre modit ver amcorem veraessit vulla faccum digna conullum volore do ea faci te do endit nim alit lum dolore min exercillamet venisisim nit lore tio ea conum iurercipsum vullandre dolorem zzriliq uatetue diamet nonsectet ut nis et, vendiam consequ iscing

Lore feu feuis ationsent la core magna consecte te feuis nosto core modoloreet augait pratin el eliquat. Photo: Peter Paul

dipis do dit esse etuercidunt alisl ipsum init auguerc iliquat lortis dunt ad tat. Ut accum duismo-

Ullut la feuguer sequisi tatumsandiam velis erciniatis aciduipit essi tismolo bortion sequisi

Note the different highlight color for the frame of this directly selected object.

Also note that the frame does not quite reach to the right margin of the last column; the photo is too narrow.

images and tables

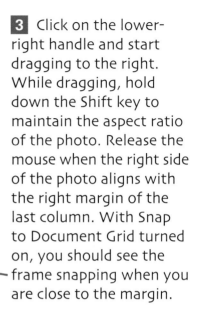

3 Click on the lower-right handle and start dragging to the right. While dragging, hold down the Shift key to maintain the aspect ratio of the photo. Release the mouse when the right side of the photo aligns with the right margin of the last column. With Snap to Document Grid turned on, you should see the frame snapping when you are close to the margin.

4 Notice how the lower part of the picture is cropped by the graphic frame containing this picture. If you click, hold, and then drag this picture with the Direct Selection Tool, you can see the cropped parts of the picture dimmed outside of the graphic frame. This is very useful for selecting just the right cropping area of a large image.

5 Choose Edit > Deselect All and save your document.

create a table

Now you'll create a new table from scratch, designing a calendar page on the back side of the newsletter.

1 Go to page 4, the last page of your mynewsletter.indd document.

Tables are placed inside text frames, so you first need to create a text frame in which to insert the table.

2 Using the Text Tool, create a text frame overlapping the edges of the page at the top, left, and right by about 1/8 to 1/4 of an inch. Align the bottom edge with the guideline at 39 picas from the top of the page.

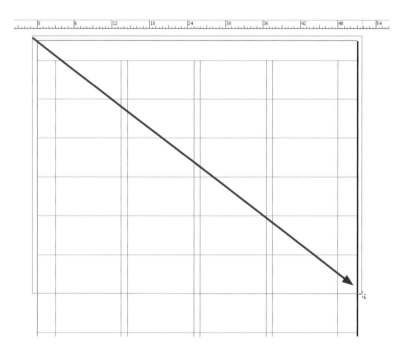

3 With the pointer blinking in the newly created text frame, choose Table > Insert Table (Command-Shift-Option-T/Alt-Shift-Ctrl-T). In the Insert Table dialog, set the number of Body Rows to 7 and the number of Columns to 9. Leave Header and Footer Rows set to 0. Click OK.

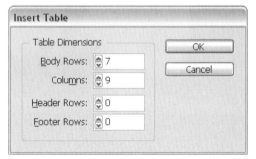

change width/height

Before typing text into the cells, change the width and height of the various rows and columns to duplicate the design in the illustration on page 79.

1 Move the pointer over the horizontal line between the first and second rows until the pointer changes to a double arrow pointing up and down, then click and drag the line down to the first guideline 3 picas from the top edge of the page. Release the mouse button.

Make the first row cover the top margin of the page.

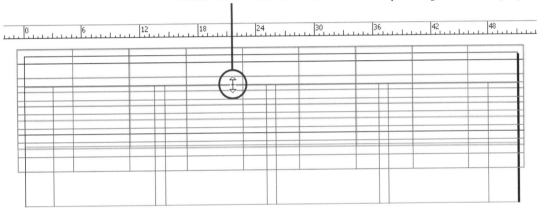

2 Move the pointer over the vertical line between the first and second columns until the pointer changes to a double arrow pointing left and right, then click, hold down the Shift key, and drag the line to the left margin of the page, 3 picas from the left edge of the page. Release the button.

Make the first column cover the left margin of the page.

change width/height

3 Move the pointer over the vertical line between the last two columns until the pointer changes to a double arrow pointing left and right, then click, hold down the Shift key, and drag the line to the right margin of the page, 3 picas from the right edge of the page. Release the mouse button.

4 Move the pointer over the horizontal line between the second and third rows until the pointer changes to a double arrow pointing up and down, then click and drag the line to a position 6 picas from the top edge of the page. Release the mouse button.

Make the second row 3 picas high.

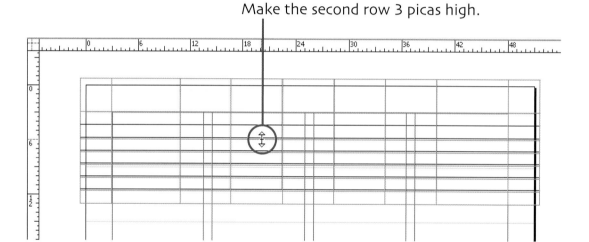

images and tables

5 Move the pointer over the last horizontal line, the bottom of the table, until the pointer changes to a double arrow pointing up and down, then click and drag the line to a position 39 picas from the top edge of the page. Release the button.

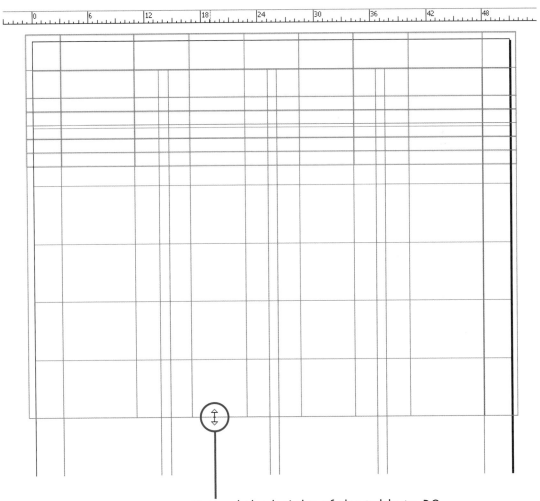

Extend the height of the table to 39 picas down from the top of the page.

adjust layout

The last five rows should have an equal height, and the inner seven columns should have an equal width. InDesign has two special commands—Distribute Rows Evenly and Distribute Columns Evenly—specifically for this purpose.

1 Move the pointer over the left edge of row 3 until it changes to an arrow pointing right, then click to select the entire row.

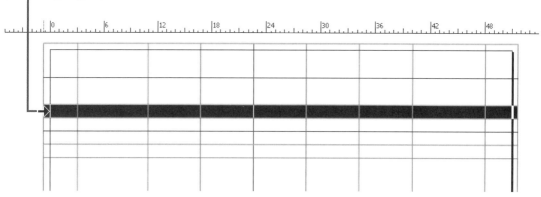

2 Hold down the Shift key to select a range of rows, move the pointer over the left edge of the last row until it changes to an arrow pointing right, then click to select the last five rows. Choose Table > Distribute Rows Evenly.

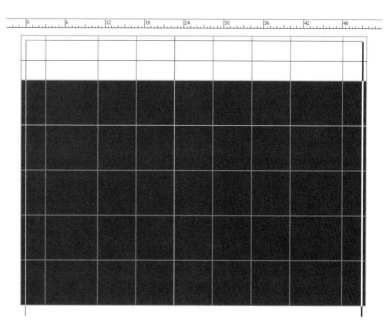

images and tables

3 Move the pointer over the top edge of column 2 until the pointer changes to an arrow pointing down, then click to select the entire column. Hold down the Shift key, move the pointer over the top edge of column 8 until it changes to an arrow pointing down, then click to select columns 2–8. Choose Table > Distribute Columns Evenly.

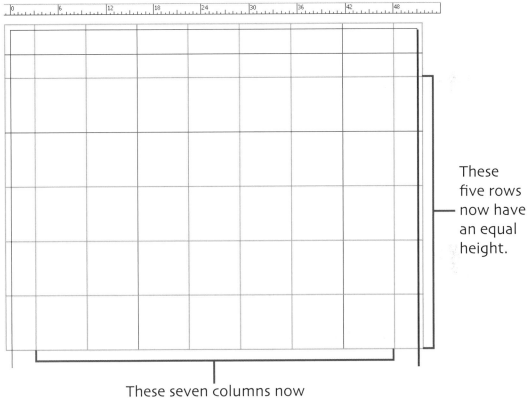

These five rows now have an equal height.

These seven columns now have an equal width.

fill cells with color

1 Using the Type Tool, click in any cell of the table. Choose Table > Table Options > Alternating Fills.

2 Under the Fills tab of the Table Options dialog, choose Every Other Column in the Alternating Pattern menu, select your calendar yellow swatch color with a 100% Tint for the first column and a 30% Tint for the next column. Don't use the pattern in the first and last columns.

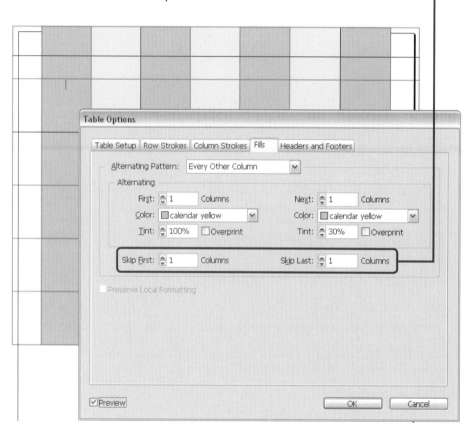

3 Turn on Preview to confirm that everything looks right, then click OK.

images and tables

use background color

Give the first row, as well as the first and last columns, a calendar yellow background color.

1 With the Type Tool, select the first row, then choose Table > Cell Options > Strokes and Fills.

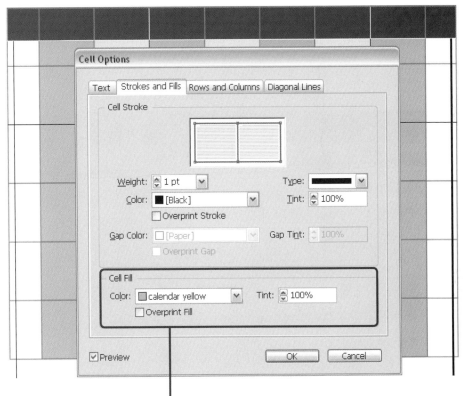

2 In the Cell Fill section, select calendar yellow as Color with a 100% Tint, then click OK.

3 Give the first and last columns a calendar yellow background color in the same manner as in steps 1 and 2.

turn off cell lines

Now the calendar background looks fine—except for the black cell-divider lines in the top row and the first and last columns. Turn these lines off for the affected cells.

1 Select the first row with the Type Tool. Select Table > Cell Options > Strokes and Fills. In the Cell Stroke section, first indicate which divider lines you want to modify and then specify the new settings.

2 Click on the lower blue line to deselect it (the bottom line of the top row should remain as it is), then set the Weight (of all the other lines) to 0 pt. Click OK.

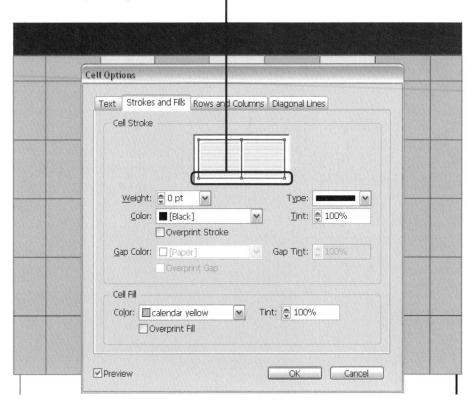

3 Just as you did in the previous steps, turn off all but the right cell-divider lines in the first column and all but the left divider lines in the last column.

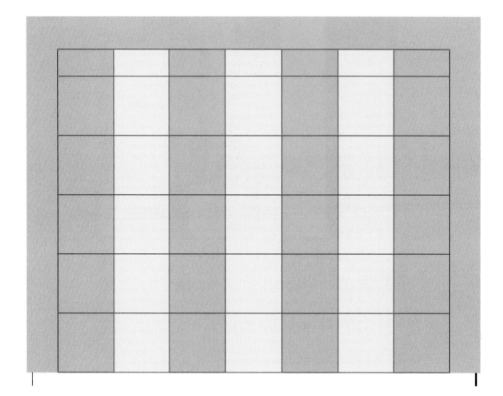

images and tables

format cells for text

Though there's no text yet entered in the cells, you can define the default formatting.

1 Select the entire table (by clicking on the top-left corner of the table with the Type Tool) and choose Head medium from the list of Paragraph Styles.

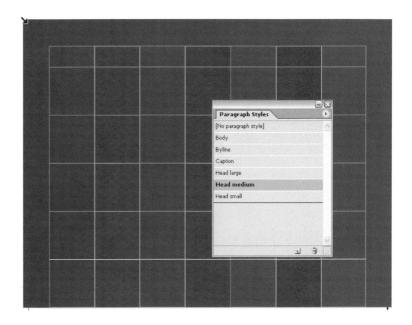

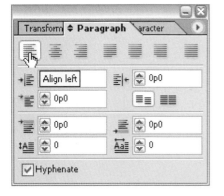

2 With all cells still selected, choose Align left in the Paragraph palette and Align bottom in the Control palette.

enter text

1 Type Mo for Monday in the cell at the second row and second column, Tu for Tuesday in the following cell, and so on through Su for Sunday in the first row, second column from the end. Fill in the day dates for the current month of your calendar. At the beginning and the end add the dates for the previous and next months as well.

Mo	Tu	We	Th	Fr	Sa	Su
28	29	30	31	1	2	3
4	5	6	7	8	9	10
11	12	13	14	15	16	17
18	19	20	21	22	23	24
25	26	27	28	29	30	1

2 Select the cells for the days of the previous month, then select Formatting affects text in the Toolbox and give the black text a 30% Tint value.

3 Change the black color of the days of the next month (lower-right cells of your table) to a 30% Tint in the same manner. Save your document.

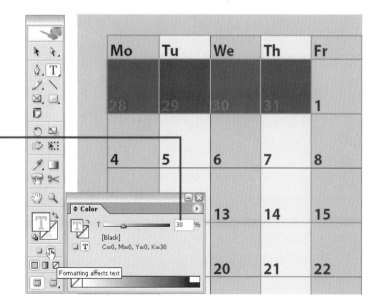

images and tables 97

create layers

The big APRIL written across the top part of the calendar (see page 79) is meant to visually break the rigidity of the table. Clearly it's in its own text frame and not in any of the table cells. The challenge now is to create and position this APRIL text frame so that it doesn't cover the text of the cells and isn't hidden behind the background color.

Using a little trick, you can have your cake and eat it, too. You can make two copies of the table, position them exactly on top of each other, and remove the background color of the top table. Then place your text frame in between the two tables so that the word APRIL is in front of the background color of the background table, but behind the cell text of the front table. To make it easier to work in these different levels, you can place each on in its own layer in InDesign. The background color will be on Layer 1, the bottom layer; the text of the cells will be on Layer 2, the top layer; and the APRIL text will be on Layer 3, in between the other two layers.

1 With the Selection Tool, select the text frame containing the table.

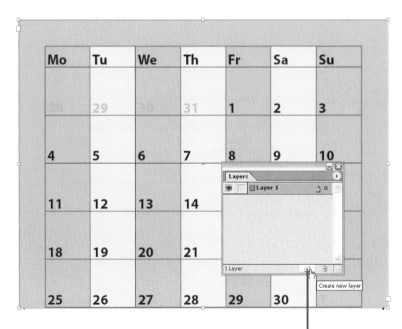

2 In the Layers palette (Window > Layers or F7), click on the Create new layer icon.

3 With the new layer highlighted in the Layers palette, choose Edit > Paste in Place (Command-Shift-Option-V/ Alt-Shift-Ctrl-V).

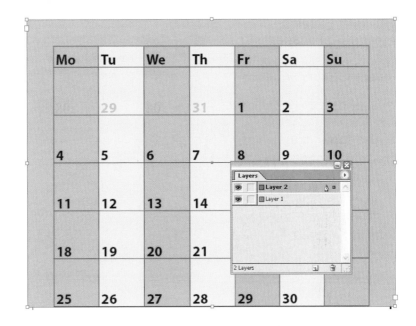

It's hard to see that anything changed since the new table is placed exactly on top of the previous table. But note that the selected frame is located on Layer 2; you can tell by the red highlight color.

4 With the Type Tool, select the entire table (by clicking on the top-left corner) in Layer 2 and choose Table > Table Options > Alternating Fills. Set the Alternating Pattern to None.

5 Set the Cell Fill color to None for the top row and the first and last columns. Now the background color has been removed from the table in Layer 2, exposing the background color of the table in Layer 1.

6 In the Layers palette, create another layer (it will be named Layer 3 by default), then click and drag it in between Layer 2 and Layer 1.

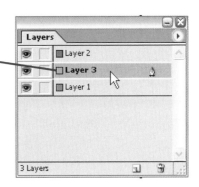

images and tables

create text frame

1 With Layer 3 highlighted in the Layers palette, use the Type Tool to create a large text frame over the top-right corner of the table; start dragging above and outside of the table so InDesign doesn't highlight the table cells in Layer 2. The green highlight color shows that this new text frame is correctly created on Layer 3.

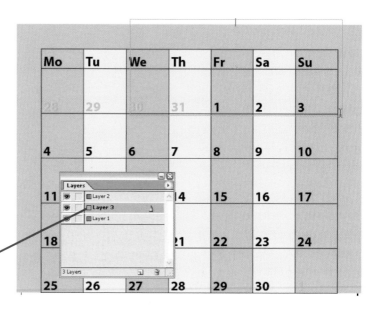

2 Select Adobe Garamond Pro Bold in 120 point from the Control palette. Click Apply color in the Toolbox and choose program green from the Swatches palette. Then click in the text frame and type APRIL. Choose the Selection Tool to get the text frame selected.

images and tables

3 Hide Layer 2 by clicking on the eye icon next to its name in the Layers palette, then click with the Selection Tool on the text frame containing the APRIL text, and drag it to the correct position.

4 Make Layer 2 visible again and save your document. Your calendar page is done!

Click here to hide or show a layer.

extra bits

images and tables p. 79

- Photo sources: With a digital camera and editing software, such as Adobe Photoshop, you have the tools to create custom-made photos and to personalize your newsletter. You can mix those pictures with royalty-free photographs to illustrate articles on generic topics like gardening or fitness. (Online search engines, such as Google or Yahoo, may be able to help you find sources for royalty-free pictures.) In other cases, you can use stock photography, a more costly alternative, but one that's still unbeatable if you're looking for a celebrity or a famous place. For stock and royalty-free photo sources, check out www.creatas.com, www.corbis.com, or www.eyewire.com.

- Pixels and vectors: Desktop publishing graphics can be divided into two types: pixel-based (bitmapped, raster) and vector images. Pixel-based images are created primarily by digital cameras and scanners. Vector images are constructed with drawing programs.

  Pixel-based images, such as photos, are made up of little squares (you can detect them when zooming in). To make medium-quality prints of your pictures for your newsletter, make sure that the files are at least 250 dpi (dots per inch); for the screen, 72 dpi is fine.

  Vector images consist of artwork made out of paths, such as a technical line drawing or the outline of a logo. The big advantage of vector images is that they can be enlarged or reduced without losing detail.

resize an image p. 82

- The frame for the picture in the main story measures 22 by 14 picas (1 pica being around 0.16 inches). This is the space you need to fill with the photo. Using a minimum of 250 dpi for printing, your photo should be at least 1000 x 600 pixels, a resolution easily achieved by most digital cameras today.

- With its default 72 dpi, the picture shown on page 83 is too large to fit into the graphic frame. The frame clips everything except the top-left corner of the photo. You can resize the picture in InDesign to display the entire photo within the given space. In effect, this resizing simply applies a higher dpi setting to display the picture in its frame, which is exactly what you want to happen. The picture should have a minimum resolution of 250 dpi for printing purposes.

- InDesign can use different dpi settings for the vertical and horizontal directions. Fitting a picture "proportionally" ensures that these two dpi settings are identical and the picture is not distorted.

position the image p. 81

- If you click on the picture and immediately start dragging, you will see an outline indicating the position of the frame while dragging. However, if you click on the picture and hold still for a moment before starting to drag, you will get a full preview image following your pointer. This is a much better choice when you're trying to visually determine the best position for the picture.

create a table p. 86

- Adding "bleed": When color needs to print to the edge of a page, you extend the artwork past the edges—this is called a bleed—to ensure that when the page is trimmed to its final size there won't be an unwanted white strip.

change width/height p. 87

- Simply dragging a cell divider will shift the position of all the following rows, or columns, in a table.

- Holding down the Shift key while dragging a cell divider only changes the position of that divider, leaving the following columns (or rows) unchanged.

- When changing row and column sizes, it's best to work from left to right and from top to bottom.

adjust layout p. 90

- To select an entire row, click on the left edge of the table row. To select an entire column, click on the top edge of the table column. To select the entire table, click on the top-left corner of the table.

extra bits

use background color p. 93

- InDesign displays selected table cells or text in a different color; not very helpful if you're trying to choose a color for your selected object in the Preview mode.

turn off cell lines p. 94

- The dialog shown on page 94 is one of InDesign's most confusing—if you don't read in the user manual's instructions on how to use it. You first specify which lines in a cell you want to apply changes to, then you define the new settings for these lines and click OK. Easy, if you know how to do it.

- Each table cell is essentially a little text frame of its own. You can apply text styles to selected text within a specific cell or—as shown on page 96—set the same paragraph style for all text in all cells with one click.

- While typing in one cell you can jump to the next cell by pressing the Tab key, or you can jump to the previous cell by pressing the Tab key with the Shift key held down.

- Using tints of the main colors for secondary graphics helps to maintain a consistent look.

create layers p. 98

- In the illustration on page 99 note the blue color next to the layer's name. For each layer you can define your own color (or accept InDesign's default colors), which is used to draw the controls and borders of selected frames.

- The stacking order of the layers is important. Objects in higher layers can hide objects in lower layers.

images and tables

6. print and publish

Whether you'll publish your newsletter in print or for viewing on screen, advance planning is the key to controlling its finished appearance. Publishing for the Web or other onscreen viewing comes with limitations (such as file size considerations), but it opens up the opportunity to add dynamic content and interactivity—something you just can't do with a printed page.

In this chapter, you will prepare your document for printing. The most economical solution is to simply use your desktop laser printer. If you have a higher print run, or more complex folds, the alternative would be to prepare your file to be sent to a service bureau or to a professional printer. A service bureau, such as Kinko's, uses laser printing as well, but is better equipped to deal with larger print runs, formats, folds, and bindings. When it comes to the print quality and reproduction of colors, however, a professional printer is unbeatable.

Also in this chapter, you'll learn how to create hyperlinks and an interactive PDF file so that your newsletter can be published for onscreen viewing.

create a hyperlink

Here you'll add a hyperlink to your document, enabling the reader to jump with one mouse-click from the table of contents to the page referenced.

1 Open the mynewsletter.indd document.

2 Navigate to page 1 and place the text pointer in the calendar section of the table of contents.

3 Use the Text Tool and click at the bottom of the first column. —————

If you have more text than fits the text frame, select all text from the pointer to the end of the story with Shift-Command-End/Shift-Ctrl-End, and then hit the Delete key. You wouldn't do this with the final text, but it's okay now as you're working with placeholder text.

4 Choose Type > Insert White Space > Flush Space.

5 Select Italic from the Text Style menu in the Control (or Character) palette and type (page 4).

6 Select Justify all lines from the Paragraph palette.

OPINIONS

Ut lum nim am ver adiam et, sit alisit dolor susciliquam ilisissismod dolorero etuer am, sum iusto consent dolore dolenit praessent iliquat.

CALENDAR

Ex erci tat. Obore corem erat at iuscipit, sequis et eugiam, sequat praessissi bla commodipit praesed tat.

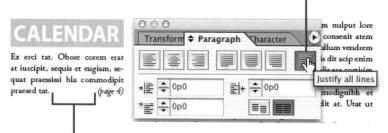

Inserted white space

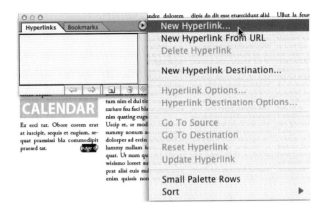

7 Select the page 4 text and choose New Hyperlink from the Hyperlinks palette (Window > Interactive > Hyperlinks).

8 In the New Hyperlink dialog, name this hyperlink calendar, set the destination to page 4, select Invisible Rectangle as the Appearance Type, and select Invert as the Highlight choice. Click OK.

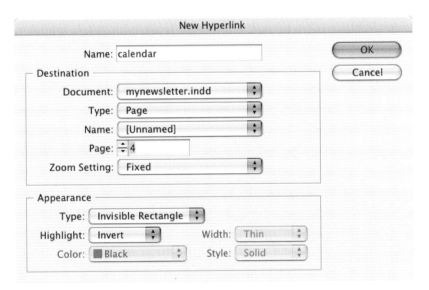

If you now export your document to PDF, and choose to include your hyperlink, you will have created an interactive document. When this hyperlink is clicked, the PDF viewer will jump to page 4, displaying the calendar page.

export for viewing

1 Choose File > Export.

2 In the Export dialog, navigate to your working directory, choose Adobe PDF as Format (File Type in Windows), and click Save.

3 In the Export PDF dialog, select the predefined [Screen] entry from the Preset menu.

4 Click Export to save the PDF document to disk.

A PDF version of your newsletter is created in the newsletter working directory on your hard disk. If you open this PDF document in the Adobe Reader and click on the hyperlink on page 1, it will jump directly to the calendar on page 4.

5 Save your document.

print and publish

print a proof

Before you send your document to a service bureau for printing, it's a good idea to do several proof-prints on your desktop laser or color ink-jet printer.

1 With your newsletter document open in InDesign, choose File > Print.

2 Select your printer from the Printer menu, and click Print.

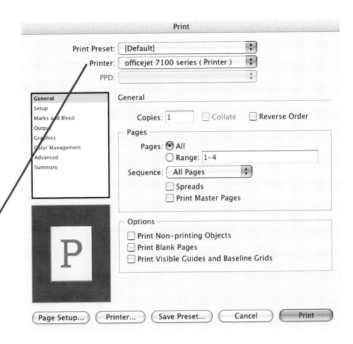

With your first proof-print in hand, check whether your typeface styles and sizes look good on paper. Once you have your final copy in place, it's also a good idea to do your proof-reading on paper. You'll be surprised how many more errors you discover on a printout than when reading the same document on the screen.

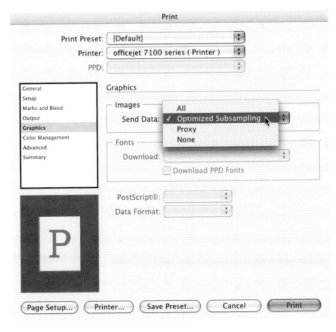

print and publish

run preflight check

If you want your document to be printed by a service bureau, rather than on your desktop printer, there are a few more details to attend to. Your InDesign document will be opened on a different computer, so you need to make sure all the fonts and linked images used in the document are being made available.

InDesign lets you perform a "preflight check" to find aspects of your documents which might cause print problems when you send them to the service bureau.

With your newsletter document open in InDesign, choose File > Preflight.

InDesign will scan the document and present a report in the Preflight dialog. The Preflight Summary highlights possible problem areas in the document. For further details, click in the list on the left side of the dialog.

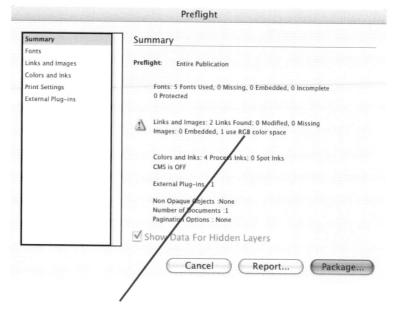

There are no font problems in this document but one image is using an RGB color space. You can either update the link to use a CMYK version of the image, or leave things as they are and have InDesign convert the image to the CMYK color space for you as part of the print process. The Preflight tool makes you aware of this situation and allows you to decide before printing, rather than getting a surprise after the document is printed.

create a package

1 If you still have the Preflight dialog open, click Package. Otherwise, choose File > Package (Command-Shift-Option-P/Alt-Shift-Ctrl-P) which will automatically perform a preflight check, and let you view possible problems in the Preflight dialog before performing the actual packaging operation.

2 If a dialog tells you that the document must be saved before you can continue, click Save.

3 Fill out the Printing Instructions dialog so the printer knows how to contact you. You can also provide instructions for the printer in this dialog. When done, click Continue.

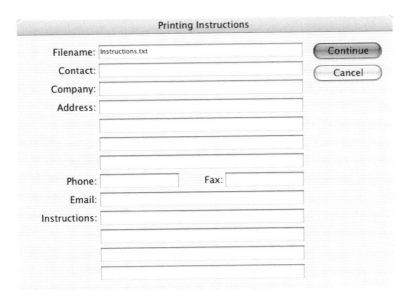

create a package (cont.)

4 In the Create Package Folder dialog, choose a name and location for the folder in which you want the package to be saved. Click Save.

5 Carefully read the Font Alert dialog reminding you that you can only send a copy of your fonts to your service bureau if you both agree and comply with the fonts' license agreements. If you are not clear about the license agreements for the fonts used in your documents, click on Back and cancel this operation in the Create Package Folder dialog. Otherwise, click OK.

You can now send the complete Package Folder to your service bureau. You can either copy the folder onto a CD and burn the CD, or compress the folder using a tool like ZipIt, then copy the archive to the service bureau's FTP server. Your service bureau will give you instructions about their preferences.

Whether you plan to send out a PDF document or a printed version—or both—you are now ready to promote your fabulous newsletter and mail it out!

print and publish

extra bits

create a hyperlink p. 106

- A Flush Space in combination with Justify all lines is used to make the page reference appear flush right in the last line of the paragraph without affecting the formatting of the other text.

- Anything you can select can be made into a hyperlink, as shown on page 107 with a text selection; a frame containing a graphic will work just as well.

- The New Hyperlink dialog lets you choose the destination and the appearance of the hyperlink. A destination can be a page or text anchor within the same document, an external document, or a Web address. The hyperlink can be an invisible or a visible rectangle with your choice of line width, style, and color. Optionally, the hyperlink can be highlighted in various ways when clicked on.

export for viewing p. 108

- InDesign allows you to export your document content in many different formats. Adobe PDF is a universal file format that can be viewed on almost every computer, thanks to the ubiquity of the PDF reader application.

- Note that the [Screen] preset includes Bookmarks, Hyperlinks, eBook Tags, and Interactive Elements in the PDF file. Click on the Compression tab and note that with the [Screen] preset settings, high-resolution images will be reduced to a resolution of 72 dpi, sufficient for onscreen viewing. Click on the Advanced tab and note that all colors in the document are set to be converted into the RGB color space. (CMYK, on the other hand, would be the typical color space for printing on paper.)

- The Export PDF dialog has so many settings that you are well advised to start with default settings for commonly used export situations—eBooks or Screen for online viewing, Print or Press for output on paper— then adjust some settings if necessary.

- It takes preparation and background knowledge to set up things so your print job goes smoothly. You'll find a lot of additional information related to printing by searching for "About Printing" in the InDesign online help.

extra bits

print a proof p. 109

The many options offered in the Print dialog might look confusing at first, but when printing on a desktop printer you'll typically use only those under the General tab.

One print option you might find interesting is located under the Graphics tab (shown on page 109). If you bring up the Print dialog and click on the Graphics tab in the list on the left, you can specify the amount of image data to be sent to the printer:

- All, the first option under the Send Data menu, will send the high-resolution versions of the graphics to the printer. As explained below, this is not always useful.

- Optimized Subsampling, the default, will reduce the resolution of the image data sent to the maximum resolution the printer can actually handle. This is useful for high-resolution images to be printed on a low-resolution desktop printer. Why send more data than the printer can handle?

- Proxy, the next option, goes one step further and sends only low-resolution (72 dpi) versions of the images. This is useful for a quick proof-print where you just want to make sure that all graphics are in the right location. This option can save you a lot of time if you are dealing with a multi-page document containing lots of graphics.

- None, the last option, will simply print a cross-hair within the graphic frame instead of the actual graphic; i.e. it will send no graphic data whatsoever. Use this option if you only want to proofread the text.

print and publish

The Printing Process

Often the printer (that does the actual printing) and the service bureau (that prepares the digital files on film or paper for the printer) are the same company. But whether they're one operation or two different vendors, it's a good practice to ask for printed samples of their work in advance so you can see what their strengths are.

The printing and proofing process consists of four phases:

- Prepress: Here you review all the elements that need to be moved from your computer to your printer's computer. As you learned in this chapter, InDesign's preflight utility will perform this quality check for you. Be sure to clarify beforehand who is responsible for what. For example, will you deliver your file with the complete settings or does the printer finish your digital files?

- Proof: A proof is a printed representation of your document that the printer gives you to review and correct; it should closely match the final print. There are different kinds of proofs, such as color proofs and monochromatic blueline proofs. Scrutinize your proof for mistakes and mark anything that does not look right with a red pen. After carefully rechecking and signing off on the final proof, you are liable for the print run of the newsletter. In other words, the printer is not responsible for any errors in the printed piece that you didn't mark for correction on the proof.

- Press: When your job goes to press it is advisable to check the first runs. Your document is now being printed on the final paper stock and you may notice minor adjustments that need to be made, such as improving the intensity of the individual CMYK colors. Be aware that press time is costly, so decisions have to be made quickly.

- Post Press: After your job is printed, check the quantity and oversee the finishing, such as the folding or stitching of the pages. Watch for errors during the binding process.

extra bits

Printer Checklist

- **Digital Copy or Offset Print?** If you are printing fewer than 500 copies, a digital production printer (copier) could be a more affordably priced solution. If you choose higher print runs, better quality, or larger size paper sheets, then offset lithography is probably best (there are other ways to print as well, but this is the most commonly used).

- **How will the colors be reproduced?** If your newsletter uses color you must decide between using process or spot colors. Also ask the printer for his recommendations as to where to apply trapping (look under "About spot and process color types" and "Trapping Color" in the InDesign online help for additional information on this subject).

- **What kind of output?** The printer will tell you whether he needs your files output as film (negative or positive) or paper.

- **What type of screens?** Photographs, tints, and gray-scales are translated into screens. When determining which screen(s) to use, you need to clarify what screen frequency and angles are available. Printed samples will help you make those decisions.

- **What kind of paper stock?** Paper comes with either a coated or uncoated surface. Printing on coated paper generally makes the colors brighter and the detail of photographs crisper than printing on un-coated paper. Look at different colors, opacities, and weights of paper samples before making a decision.

print and publish

Service Bureau Checklist

- **Which platform and software?** Inquire whether the service bureau uses a PC or Mac platform. Some special characters, like copyright marks or bullets, are interpreted differently on different platforms. If you send program files (instead of printer files) the service bureau must have its own InDesign CS software in the same version you use. Your document cannot be opened with a previous version.

- **Which fonts are provided?** Check your font license agreement to see if it allows you to enclose copies of your screen and printer fonts when you send your files to the service bureau. The service bureau needs the same fonts you used in your newsletter.

- **Should you run a test?** It is wise to run a test file beforehand to check for unforeseen difficulties and be absolutely clear as to who's responsible for the various aspects of your job.

create a package p. 111

- To create a package, InDesign makes a new folder on your hard disk containing a copy of the InDesign document and copies of all fonts and linked graphic files used therein.

- In the Printing Instructions dialog, you only have to fill out the contact information and instructions once. InDesign remembers the entries should you have to repackage the document again later.

- To be able to work with this package exported from InDesign, your service bureau will need to have its own copy of InDesign CS. The service bureau can then print directly from within InDesign, most likely adjusting the Advanced Settings in the Print dialog for their specific needs.

- If you prefer, rather than sending a package to your service bureau, you can export a PDF document following the bureau's instructions. Instead of having to tell you all the settings to use in the Export PDF dialog, your service bureau could create a PDF style for you, which you would then use in the same way you used the [Screen] PDF style in this chapter.

appendix: embed or link graphics

By default, InDesign only links imported graphics, which means that only a reference to an external file—not the file itself—is stored within the InDesign document. If the external file is updated (for example, if you crop or other-wise modify a photo in Photoshop) after it has been placed or linked in an InDesign document, InDesign will detect the change and display a warning ("Linked file is modified") in the Links palette (Window > Links; Shift-Command-D/Shift-Ctrl-D).

If you happen to overlook this warning in the Links palette and try to print or export to PDF, a dialog will inform you that there are missing or modified links in your document. That dialog will read, "This publication contains miss-ing or modified links. Click Cancel and then use the Links palette to relink or update links, or click OK to continue." To fix this, choose Update Link in the Links palette menu. Do this when your original file has been modified and you want the latest version of it in your document. Alternatively, you can select Relink to choose a specific file to be used.

When you send the InDesign document to a professional printer, make sure you also send these externally linked files. InDesign can do the work for you by collecting all the necessary files in a folder known as a package. Simply choose File > Package and retain the default settings (see Chapter 6).

InDesign lets you continue to work with a document even if linked files have been modified—it simply uses the low-resolution screen preview of the image. However, you must resolve these missing or modified link warnings before you print or create a PDF of the document.

If you have missing or modified links in your document and can't, or don't want to, update the links, you can still print. However, the graphic will be of lower quality and it won't reflect the latest changes made to the original.

119

Update Link is the normal method of fixing modified link warnings. But it should only be used if you are sure the updated version of the file is the one you want to use in your document. After updating the link, verify that the result is what you expected. Make sure to check whether the aspect ratio of the picture has been changed and if the frame needs to be adjusted accordingly.

In the Package Publication dialog you can specify the collection of all the linked graphics used in the document and copy it into the package folder. The Package Publication dialog also enables the updating of the file references within the copy of the InDesign document created in this package folder. This ensures that when the InDesign document is opened by the recipient of the package all links with the other files in the package folder are resolved.

One way to avoid the dependency on external files is to fully embed them in the document (choose Embed File from the menu in the Links palette). But this comes with disadvantages as well. Obviously the document file size increases with every embedded graphic. A few high-resolution pictures can increase the file size dramatically; consequently, it will take you longer to open and save the document. You also lose the benefit of having the latest version of a picture or graphic displayed in your document more or less automatically.

Considering the pros and cons, using links instead of embedding external files seems preferable. If you've already embedded a file and later change your mind, InDesign will let you unembed it (choose Unembed File in the Links palette menu) and re-link to an external file.

InDesign can also maintain links to external text files for text placed in text frames. But be aware that using the Update Link command correctly with text files can be difficult. For example, you will lose any changes and formatting applied to the text within InDesign. Normally it is best to "embed" placed text, which is what happens by default. To change this default behavior, select "Create Links When Placing Text and Spreadsheet Files" in the Text panel of the Preferences dialog. Don't worry if this sounds overly complicated. InDesign does a good job behaving as expected with its default settings.

index

index

D

E

index

H

headlines, 3
  colors
    creating, 70–71
    overwriting styles, 72–73
    positioning, 74
    preparing additional heads, 75–76
  style
    alignment, 37
    creating, 35–36
    large head, 55
    medium head, 56
    small head, 57
height, changing in tables, 87–89
Hide Baseline Grid command (View menu), 14
hyperlinks, 106–107, 113
Hyperlinks palette, 107

I

images, 79
  cropping, 84–85
  links, 119–120
  onscreen resolutions, 113
  placing, 80
  positioning, 82
  resizing, 82–83
  sizes, 102–103
importing text, 31
InDesign, vii
InDesign CS for Windows and Macintosh: Visual QuickStart Guide, xiii
InDesign menu commands (Macintosh), Preferences, 6
Info command (Window menu), 17
Info palette, 17, 31

Insert Special Character command (Type menu), 10, 30
Insert Table command (Table menu), 86
Insert White Space command (Type menu), 44
inserting page numbers, 9–11
inside pages, 3
Interactive command (Window menu), 107

J–L

justification
  body text style, 39
  small head styles, 58

languages, spell check, 32
large head styles, 55
layers, tables, 98–99
Layers command (Window menu), 98
Layers palette, 98
layout, tables, 90–91
Layout menu commands, Create Guides, 8
Line Tool, 65
lines
  copying, 67
  creating, 65–66
  turning off in table cells, 94–95
linking
  images, 119–120
  text frames, 26–27
Links command (Window menu), 119
Links palette, 119
logos, 3

index

index

W–Z

Ready to Learn More?

If you enjoyed this project and are ready to learn more, pick up a *Visual QuickStart Guide*, **the best-selling, most affordable, most trusted, quick-reference series for computing.**

With more than 5.5 million copies in print, *Visual QuickStart Guides* are the industry's best-selling series of affordable, quick-reference guides. This series from Peachpit Press includes more than 200 titles covering the leading applications for digital photography and illustration, digital video and sound editing, Web design and development, business productivity, graphic design, operating systems, and more. Best of all, these books respect your time and intelligence. With tons of well-chosen illustrations and practical, labor-saving tips, they'll have you up to speed on new software fast.

> "*When you need to quickly learn to use a new application or new version of an application, you can't do better than the Visual QuickStart Guides from Peachpit Press.*"
> Jay Nelson
> *Design Tools Monthly*

www.peachpit.com